Rescue Ink

Rescue Ink

HOW TEN GUYS SAVED

COUNTLESS DOGS AND CATS,

TWELVE HORSES, FIVE PIGS, ONE DUCK,

AND A FEW TURTLES

Rescue Ink

with Denise Flaim

VIKING

VIKING
Published by the Penguin Group
Penguin Group (USA) Inc., 375 Hudson Street, New York, New York 10014, U.S.A.
Penguin Group (Canada), 90 Eglinton Avenue East, Suite 700, Toronto, Ontario,
Canada M4P 2Y3 (a division of Pearson Penguin Canada Inc.)
Penguin Books Ltd, 80 Strand, London WC2R 0RL, England
Penguin Ireland, 25 St. Stephen's Green, Dublin 2, Ireland
(a division of Penguin Books Ltd)
Penguin Books Australia Ltd, 250 Camberwell Road, Camberwell, Victoria 3124,
Australia (a division of Pearson Australia Group Pty Ltd)
Penguin Books India Pvt Ltd, 11 Community Centre, Panchsheel Park,
New Delhi – 110 017, India
Penguin Group (NZ), 67 Apollo Drive, Rosedale, North Shore 0632, New Zealand
(a division of Pearson New Zealand Ltd)
Penguin Books (South Africa) (Pty) Ltd, 24 Sturdee Avenue, Rosebank,
Johannesburg 2196, South Africa

Penguin Books Ltd, Registered Offices: 80 Strand, London WC2R 0RL, England

First published in 2009 by Viking Penguin, a member of Penguin Group (USA) Inc.

1 3 5 7 9 10 8 6 4 2

Copyright © Rescue Ink Publications LLC, 2009
All rights reserved

LIBRARY OF CONGRESS CATALOGING IN PUBLICATION DATA
Flaim, Denise.
Rescue Ink : how ten guys saved countless dogs and cats, twelve horses, five pigs,
one duck, and a few turtles / Rescue Ink with Denise Flaim.
p. cm.
ISBN 978-0-670-02116-1
1. Animal rescue. I. Rescue Ink. II. Title.
HV4708.F583 2009
179'.3—dc22   2009018185

Printed in the United States of America
Designed by Nancy Resnick

Dedicated to all the animals who have been saved
from the cruel hands of abusers,
and to those for whom help was too late

There is much more work to be done.

Contents

Rescue Ink

1

Clara

Bulldog Meets Alpha Dogs

*M*ilk for the baby, a few containers of yogurt, something for tomorrow's breakfast.

While running over her mental shopping list, Jessica Kurland tied her three-and-a-half-year-old bulldog, Clara, to a railing outside the Food Emporium on Forty-third Street and Tenth Avenue in Manhattan. It was mid-March of 2008, a week before Easter, and pitch-dark at 8:30 P.M. But it was a long elevator ride up to her thirty-first-floor apartment to drop Clara off. And she'd be in the store only a few minutes. Besides, Jessica wasn't the only one who had interrupted her dog-walking for a quick dash through the dairy aisle; another dog was tied to the rail, waiting patiently for an owner who had disappeared beyond the thump of the glass doors.

But when Jessica came back out of the supermarket five minutes later, she didn't register the flash of red that was Clara's leash. Startled, she stared at the spot where her wrinkle-faced, wriggle-bottomed bulldog should have been patiently waiting.

It was empty. Nothing but bare concrete and the whoosh of nearby bus exhaust. No Clara.

Panic-stricken, Jessica looked up and down the street, hoping to see Clara's charming waddle among the jumble of legs. As the stream of passersby marched on, so did the creeping fear in Jessica's chest. Her dog was gone without a trace.

"I started running up and down the sidewalks, screaming her name," remembers Jessica, who instinctively knew that Clara had not wandered off. She never strayed, even when off leash. "I was grabbing people: 'Have you seen a bulldog?'"

Jessica cruised around in a police car for an hour and a half as the officers scoured the neighborhood, hoping for a glimpse of the missing dog. But after seeing no trace of her beloved Clara, she headed to a twenty-four-hour copy center, where she printed five hundred flyers with Clara's picture, her phone number, and the promise of a $3,000 reward.

Desperate to get the word out, Jessica contacted a friend, model Beth Ostrosky, the then-fiancée of shock jock Howard Stern and a devoted bulldog owner. Two days after Clara's disappearance, her story was on the air and in the city's consciousness. Marlboro-puffing truck drivers, harried commuters, bored office workers, anyone within range of Stern's Sirius satellite channel knew about the smush-faced purebred who had been lifted from a Manhattan street corner. And they knew about the newly upped $5,000 reward being offered for her safe return.

Another day passed, but still, no Clara.

Of the many breeds humans have created over the centuries, bulldogs are one of the most dramatic: With their anvil-size heads, jutting underbites, and bulky, pear-shaped bodies, they attract attention wherever they go. Bred centuries ago as the centerpiece of one of the most brutal blood sports ever devised—bull baiting, where the bulldog latched on to the nose of the enraged steer and hung on until it had drowned the bull in its own blood—the bulldog we know today exists only to be a cuddly, goofy, placid companion. So ugly they are cute, so extreme they have universal appeal, bulldogs are a breed that defies conventional wisdom.

"People think bulldogs are kind of fierce, but they're really lovers," confides Jessica, who soon encountered a group of rough-and-ready Good Samaritans who fit a similar profile. Like Clara, these animal rescuers were an equally unlikely juxtaposition of opposites: softhearted and street-smart, charming and intimidating, quick to laugh and just as quick to anger, too.

As Clara's disappearance stretched into its third day, word of the bulldog's theft had spread all over craigslist. Jessica fielded an e-mail from a retired New York City police detective named Angel Nieves. He belonged to a group of animal rescuers, he explained. "I spoke to my team, and we want to investigate and try our best to recover your dog," he wrote.

"Yes!" Jessica wrote back. She would take whatever help she could get.

And what she got was more than she ever bargained for. Never mind the stereotype of the crazy cat lady in tennis shoes feeding kittens out of pie tins in a vacant lot: Jessica was about to meet a new breed of rescuer, one that was male, macho, and not inclined to take no for an answer.

The morning after Angel's call, Jessica opened her door to a group of six men who looked like a *Sopranos* casting call at a Harley-Davidson dealership. Tattoos covered their well-muscled arms, necks, even faces, running the metaphysical gamut from praying angels to wing-spread bats. Their wardrobe was straight out of a Sturgis biker rally: denim, leather, motorcycle boots, black sweatshirts embroidered with their names in white block letters: "Batso." "G." "Big Ant." "Johnny O."

Jessica recalls her husband's reaction succinctly. "Holy shit," he said under his breath as the men crossed the threshold.

But his wife felt the stirrings of possibility. "I was so hopeful when I saw them," Jessica says. "They looked like they meant business."

They certainly did. Clara was about to become the pet project of Rescue Ink.

No one can quite pinpoint the moment when the germ of an idea about a bunch of burly, hot-rod-riding rescuers, whose arms boast more ink than a Catholic-school penmanship class, ever came to be in the first place. Robert Misseri, the group's cofounder, whose noticeably uninked appearance dovetails nicely with his daytime vocation as a Manhattan-based caterer, says the defining moment came in June of 2007.

Robert gathered a handful of guys who knew each other from hot-rod shows, tattoo parlors, motorcycle rallies, or their neighborhoods at a Midtown Chinese restaurant called Ginger's. All of them had saved animals over the years, bringing home stray cats or trying to save a chained-up dog whose owners neglected him. They just never knew that what they did had a label: animal rescue. Neither had any of them ever thought to formally band together to try to help animals, though it was only logical that a group of badass animal lovers could do more collectively than individually.

Years back, Anthony Missano, the group's gentle giant at

320 pounds, confronted someone in his Long Island neighborhood who had been seen repeatedly kicking and yelling at his dog while walking him.

"Everyone in the neighborhood knew about it for a while, but there's only so much you can take," says Big Ant. "It wasn't necessary, what he was doing to the dog."

Not one but six guys answered the door when Big Ant rang the bell.

"I said, 'Listen, everybody knows you're hurting your dog,'" Big Ant remembers. "'If you don't want him, I'll take him.'"

They hurled a few choice words, issued sundry threats, then slammed the door in his face.

A few days later, a dozen Harleys roared to a stop in front of the home of the mistreated hound mix.

At this second overture, "they took a different tone," says Big Ant with satisfaction. Maybe he didn't have time to care for the dog after all, the suddenly humbled owner suggested. So Big Ant struck a deal: If he could find a good home for the dog, the man would consider giving him up. In a few weeks, through word of mouth, a loving new home for the pooch was found.

"Everybody has a spot in their hearts for the animals," says Ant, drawing out the last word in his characteristic way, as if pulling a piece of saltwater taffy. "You don't beat down a defenseless animal. Never."

Based on that formula—a concern for animals, a crew of tough guys, and the willingness, even eagerness, to knock on a door without being afraid of what awaits beyond it—the core Rescue Ink group was formed. Of course there was Big Ant, whose cherry-red hot rod has a license plate that reads, ominously, EVILSLED. There was Joe Panzarella, who has arms the size of most people's thighs and a finely tuned sense of loyalty. And there was Johnny O, a martial-arts artist and proud owner of Lucy, a brindled pit bull who, it seems, never got the memo that she belongs to one of the nation's most maligned and supposedly vicious breeds. (Though there's probably some truth to that: given the chance, she just might lick you to death.)

At that Manhattan sit-down over lo mein with Robert, this core group talked about their outrage over a recent local news story. Across the river, on suburban Long Island where some of the guys lived, a pit bull named Maximus had been tied to a tree and set on fire. The fifty-five-pound dog had puncture wounds on his neck and the unmistakable smell of gasoline on what was left of his fur when animal control came to investigate. Though he was covered with second- and third-degree burns on more than half his body, he brought the hard-bitten animal-care officers to tears when he licked their hands and wagged his tail through the excruciating pain he was suffering.

Sadly, Maximus did not survive, though his twenty-two-year-old owner was eventually arrested for animal cruelty. But rather than giving the Rescue Ink guys closure, that ending only fueled their anger toward animal abusers, and increased their desire to see something done about them.

By the fall of 2007, work on a Web site had begun. A tattoo artist came up with the Gothic-inspired logo, the sinuous white letters of RESCUE INK standing out against a stark black background. Then came the image of a pit bull puppy with an oversize collar emblazoned with the group's name hanging around his neck, forecasting the legacy he was hoping to grow into.

As word about the group grew, so did its ranks. Rescue

Ink expanded to include a new wave of recruits: George Perry, ubiquitously known as "G," a dog-savvy landscaper from Connecticut who gets grief from the rest of the guys about his Japanese bike, a Hayabusa (though its sheer speed is his best retort). Batso, a septuagenarian biker with bats tattooed on his shaved head who makes his own soap from oatmeal and honey. Angel Nieves, the retired police detective from the Bronx who does a mean merengue. And Des Calderon, a feral-cat specialist from Harlem in camo pants and skull rings.

Without much background on the history and state of the local rescue scene, the newly cast Rescue Ink began to reach out to local rescue groups, most of which are almost by definition run by women who, at first, didn't know what to do with a bunch of eager guys who had muscle to spare. And while some of the guys may have said "spaded" instead of "spayed," and thought at first that TNR was a new cable channel instead of the shorthand cat rescuers use for "trap, neuter, and return," their hearts—and their hands—were in the right place. The guys trapped cats, built doghouses for those who could not afford them, and delivered pet food to elderly owners who went without food themselves so their dogs and cats could eat.

But Rescue Ink soon found its real niche: While most rescuers focused on solving the symptoms of animal neglect and abuse—from spaying and neutering cat colonies to finding loving homes for abandoned animals—no one was getting to the root of the problem. No one—not the police, not animal-welfare agencies, and certainly not the rescue groups—were dealing with the abusers themselves. No one had the guts to go to the drug dealers, the puppy millers, the trappers, torturers, and garden-variety dirtbags, and say, No. No, you're not going to do this to these animals anymore. And if you do, you're going to have to answer to someone; you're going to have to answer to us.

"We're not a gang, vigilantes, or a social organization, but we do have that certain 'in your face' style when it comes to animal abusers," the group explains on their Web site, the home page of which is bisected with yellow "Caution" tape that warns, "Coming to an Abuser Near You." Though Rescue Ink doesn't go into a situation with the intention of things getting physical, the guys' general attitude toward life—"You talkin' to me?"—guarantees that if they find themselves in such a situation, they're not inclined to bluff. And while they're not looking for trouble, they're ready for it if it comes.

But they're also not looking to pick a fight. Joe Panz calls the philosophy "peace through superior firepower. Like when the navy parks a ship near some pain-in-the-ass country. We give them a moment of pause and the guy thinks, 'I might get my ass kicked in front of my wife. These guys might pull my clothes off and duct-tape me to a tree. Or pour honey on me and let the dogs out.' Once you stop the bull from charging, you won," he continues. "Because now the bull's thinking, 'I forgot what I'm mad about.' Now we're talking, we're not arguing anymore."

Lost causes are Rescue Ink's specialty: a cat stranded atop a sixty-foot-tall tree. A duck separated from its flock in a drainage ditch. A family of pigs whose elderly owner can no longer care for them. A Rottweiler left to slowly starve in a suburban backyard. There are probably many rescue groups out there with more experience and tenure than this bunch of tough talkers who make regular stops on the road to rescue not only helpless animals, but also the occasional triple-decker sandwich from the clutches of the nearest Greek diner. But there probably aren't many whose appearance alone prompts police to request a backup SWAT-style team when they respond to a call from a homeowner freaked out at the muscle power gathered on his front lawn.

"We like it when the abusers call the police, because we've got nothing to hide, and we're following the law," notes founding member Johnny O. "It also puts them on the cops' radar screen—and that's what we want."

While Rescue Ink is definitely a "guy thing," that's not to say that everyone involved with the group is riding in the express lane of the testosterone highway. Mary Fayet joined Rescue Ink in early 2008 to field and help to prioritize e-mails; being the mother of three boys prepared her for the group's locker-room mentality. ("My lunch was bigger than that," says Big Ant in mock disgust at Mary's ten-pound rescued Maltese, Luigi.)

Bruce Feinberg is Rescue Ink's coordinator; when someone can't find a phone number, needs to arrange a spay-neuter, or wants to pass on the name of a potential volunteer, he usually gets the call. With his wiry frame and an irrepressible tendency to use words like "milieu," he is, he admits, the "runt of the litter." Bruce recalls his first encounter with Joe Panz at a shelter fund-raiser where he held a puppy for Joe while he removed his jacket.

"Give me back the puppy, or I'll break your arms," Joe ordered.

"You're going to have to make a wish first," Bruce replied cheerily.

"We are who we are," shrugs Joe at the memory of meeting Bruce.

And who exactly is it that they are? At the heart of it, just a bunch of animal lovers—with an edge.

"Let me put it to you this way," says Joe, cracking his knuckles in concentration. "When you were a kid walking with your father in the neighborhood, and there was a bunch of guys hanging out in front of the candy store, he made you cross the street. And when you asked why, he said, 'Because they're bad guys.' And you said, 'If they're bad guys, why don't you call the police?' And he said, 'Because they're our bad guys.'"

New Yorkers are defined by their neighborhoods, and Jessica Kurland's is known by the vivid label Hell's Kitchen. Established by Irish immigrants who built shantytowns along the Hudson River in the mid-1800s, this western slice of Midtown has a colorful history of iron-fisted Irish gangs, flamboyant bootleggers, and taciturn longshoremen. The tuneful but violent ballads of gang strife in *West Side Story* are Hell's Kitchen set to music.

In the 1980s the gritty neighborhood began to gentrify, the actors and loft dwellers from neighboring Chelsea migrated uptown in search of cheaper rents, and real-estate agents started calling the area Clinton in the hopes that it would stick. But the old-timers and the neighborhood toughs still call it Hell's Kitchen. And to the people Rescue Ink needed to reach in order to help piece together the puzzle of Clara's disappearance, Clinton ain't nothing but a president.

At first glance, it seemed that Clara had disappeared into the night, vanished without a trace. But street guys like Rescue Ink knew that there was a vibrant underworld operating on those Manhattan streets. The right inquiries asked in the

right tone of voice would provide the leads they were looking for.

Their first stop was the local homeless shelter. "We went
around and told them we were looking for this dog, and that
there was a cash reward. We said, 'Look, here, the cash is right
here, just tell us where she is,'" says Ant, patting his pocket.
But none of Hell's Kitchen's homeless had seen portly little
Clara.

The next stops were the street corners where all the neighborhood kids hung out.

"We uncovered a wealth of crime just by looking for this
dog," says Robert. "One guy said, 'Yo, I just sell nickel bags
here.' Another said, 'I'm just into car radios—I don't mess with
dogs.' If we were cops, we would have made a hundred busts."

Dog snatchings like Clara's aren't usually premeditated,
Robert says. But these crimes of opportunity give the criminals an advantage in that all the blame can be put on the victim. "A radio can't have gotten up and walked away or broke
off its leash," Robert explains. "And that's their excuse: The
dog got off its leash. Very rarely will they actually be charged
with stealing a dog."

As Rescue Ink made its rounds, a neighborhood kid started
following the guys, offering his help, which made them peg
him immediately for a snitch. He was trying to see how much
they knew, how strong their resolve was, and what their intentions were. With an intentional exuberance, the guys told him
their work had just begun; they'd be banging on doors, asking
uncomfortable questions, and putting the heat on in the neighborhood for as long as it took. So whoever the lowlife was who
stole this pricey dog in the hopes of turning around and selling
it for a couple of hundred bucks wasn't getting a reprieve.

Jessica also told Rescue Ink that, through the neighborhood grapevine, several people had intimated that an alleged puppy mill nearby was involved in selling dogs on the wholesale level. Were they somehow involved in Clara's disappearance?

Rescue Ink called on the proprietor. "We told him straight out if he was behind this, we would make it very difficult for him to run his operations and we would put pressure on him," Robert says. "He said that he had nothing to do with the crime on that side of the city"—implying that somehow Manhattan's crime was zoned as stringently as its commerce.

No lead was left unexplored: Rescue Ink even took a couple of hours to check out the predictions of a psychic who had been in touch with Jessica. While the psychic described a particular building and its residents with eerie precision, Clara was nowhere to be found in that location.

Thanks to Rescue Ink's efforts on the earthly plane, at least, the squeeze was starting to work. The day after Rescue Ink arrived on the scene, and four days after Clara's disappearance, Jessica got the phone call she had been waiting for.

"A guy called and said, 'I think my son has your dog,'" she remembers. "'We just want to return her, no questions asked, and we want to make this quick.'"

The Rescue Ink guys were out on another rescue on Long Island. Jessica was on her own for the moment.

"Where is the dog now?" she asked.

"Connecticut," came the reply—more than an hour north of Manhattan.

As instructed, Jessica and her husband waited in front of the son's apartment, only blocks from their own, until the father and son pulled up. The older man was immaculately dressed.

"So well dressed that even in New York he stood out," Jessica remembers.

Inside the car was Clara, seemingly unruffled by her four-day adventure.

"I hugged the kid and thanked him, but he was very cold and asked where the reward money was," Jessica said. With both men insisting—at increasingly higher decibels—that they had earned the $5,000 reward, the Kurlands walked with Clara to their bank branch in Times Square, the two men following closely behind them. At the ATM, they punched in $1,000—the maximum they were permitted to withdraw.

Feeling like something wasn't quite right about these guys, Jessica dialed Robert on her cell phone to get his commonsense read of the situation: "If they're good people and they really just found your dog, they're not going to want anything." For his part, Robert doubts whether Clara ever left Hell's Kitchen, and whether the two men were even related. He also wonders whether the kid that had been tailing Rescue Ink all day was friendly with the so-called son.

"You need to give him his money!" Jessica says the supposed father screamed at her. "You need to teach my son that there are still honest people in this world."

Jessica handed her cell phone with Robert on the line to the older man. "I told him he was in possession of stolen property, and he wasn't getting any rewards," Robert says. "I told him he had these people really nervous, and I was sending a guy over to help straighten things out."

Sensing that trouble was about to arrive, the scammers suddenly lost interest in their reward and left empty-handed. And the Kurlands returned home with what they considered priceless: their Clara.

Clara was the case that put Rescue Ink on the map: The *New York Post* followed the story breathlessly. More media attention followed, from local news channels and the staid *New York Times* to celebrity-crammed *People* magazine and *The Ellen DeGeneres Show*. Everybody wanted to know what makes a bunch of tattoo-loving New York City toughs use their muscle and their influence to rap on the doors of animal abusers, march against puppy mills, and stay up until all hours trapping feral cats and building doghouses for owners too poor to buy them.

And the answer is simple enough: Because they can.

While Clara brought Rescue Ink intense media attention, she didn't bring them many more members, though there have been plenty of wannabes. "People call up all the time and say, 'I got a tattoo . . . what do I have to do to join the group?'" Robert says.

But becoming a part of Rescue Ink is not about the tribal-Celtic on your calf or the skulls and roses on your pecs. Becoming part of Rescue Ink means joining a serious fraternity in which commitment, loyalty, and a willingness to be "in your face"—within the confines of the law—are necessities. So is a thick skin; belonging to this knock-around crew means taking the inevitable jokes, pranks, and teasing like a man. Rescue Ink is likely the only rescue group where colleagues will call each other "ghetto Smurf," or ask whether "syntax" is something you pay a prostitute. Like most packs, this one considers itself only as strong as its weakest member. And to join, a person needs to be considered the real deal, both in terms of his street cred and his genuine love for animals.

"We all have different personalities and professions," says Johnny O, a perfect example of one of Rescue Ink's many dichotomies; trained in martial arts and theoretically able to send you to your maker with a mere finger jab, he also went to cooking school and wears a pair of straitlaced eyeglasses that earned him the nickname Clark Kent. "Beyond the tattoos, the one common denominator is our love of animals. Don't even think past that, because that's as far as you need to go."

Since Rescue Ink started officially rescuing as a group in spring 2008, a couple of guys have dropped out, and only one more has joined the team: Eric Olsen, who first learned about this local group of tattooed rescuers when he took his miniature pinscher to an agility class. What gained Eric admittance to Rescue Ink's inner circle wasn't the tattoo of a fierce Rottweiler on his arm. It was the fact that he occasionally drives six hours round trip to Maine to visit the dog that inspired that inked tribute. He was, the guys concluded, the real deal.

There's a mission here amid the bawdy humor and seat-of-your-pants activism. "Twenty years ago, people used to drink and drive all the time. The perception of getting into a car after you had too much to drink wasn't so bad," Robert explains. "Today it's totally taboo. We want to do the same with animal abuse: We want to get society to the place where it's taboo to abuse and mistreat animals."

As for the poster girl for Rescue Ink's street-smart success, Clara is no longer a Manhattanite. Soon after her abduction, the Kurlands moved to suburban New Jersey, where their bulldog now has a big fenced backyard in which to run and play, never for a moment out of Jessica's sight.

Rescue Ink, however, has no plans to go anywhere. A year after Clara's storybook recovery, the guys are still doing what they do so well—flexing muscles, meting out one-liners, and turning stony and quiet when they run up on the doorstep of someone suspected of abuse or neglect. On their wish list is a place they can make their headquarters, where they can meet, plan, build dog and cat houses, foster animals, and even page through the occasional hot-rod magazine in their down time.

"Some days we'll meet up in front of a Dunkin' Donuts, and the police will show up and ask us what we're up to," Ant says. "And we'll say to the cop, 'We're just having a rescue meeting.'" And the cop will say, with a nod to the nervous clerk behind the counter inside, "That's the problem. He thinks you're having a meeting about the best way to rescue some of his cash."

Clara's story ended happily, but she was only the beginning. Today Rescue Ink's days are filled with saving battle-scarred pit bulls with temperaments as soft as butter and scruffy street cats who long to be lap warmers. And like their often rough-and-tumble rescuers, with this bunch it's not always wise to judge a book by its cover.

2

Johnny O

For Pits' Sake

*S*ay hello, Gracie.

The beautifully marked brindled pit bull was so elegantly built, it looked like she had whippet in her family tree.

When Johnny O first saw Gracie in April 2008, she reminded him of Lucy, his own brindled pit bull who just a few months before had introduced him to this much-misunderstood breed. The big difference, though, was that Lucy was cared for and loved, and Gracie appeared to be anything but.

A caller had given Rescue Ink a tip that a pit bull was tied up behind a split-level ranch in Long Island, with no shelter, little water or food, and a tether so short she had no room to do much more than turn around and lie down. Sitting in the garbage-strewn backyard amid bundles of wire and scraps of gutter metal, one-year-old Gracie was malnourished and neglected—a bad start to a life that was bound only to get worse.

The whole Rescue Ink crew had turned out for this case, from G, who typically on these runs is a man of few words, to Joe, who never runs out of them.

Big Ant rang the doorbell, and a sixteen-year-old girl answered the door. Patiently, the Rescue Ink guys explained that Gracie needed shelter, to which the girl responded by showing them the garage where Gracie was kept at night and in bad weather tied to a pole with no blanket over the concrete floor. Because her family did not feel secure in their somewhat rough neighborhood, she explained, they got her for "protection."

As Johnny lingered in the backyard, playing with an exuberant Gracie, Angel spoke to the teenager's mother in Spanish, explaining that Gracie needed a roof over her head, better-quality food, and regular veterinary care—she had never been vaccinated or spayed.

"She was a very high-strung dog who liked to jump on you," says Johnny, whose look—ski cap, baggy pants, and goatee—is perhaps best described as "coffeehouse biker." Gracie's high energy only contributed to a vicious cycle: Because she seemed out of control, the family was reluctant to play and interact with her, and in turn, because Gracie was starved for affection, she responded even more manically when she finally did receive attention. Eventually, Big Ant suggested that the family consider giving Gracie to a home that could better care for her.

"Then the girl started crying and saying, 'We love our dog,'" Johnny O remembers.

Softening, Big Ant explained that Rescue Ink had brought a doghouse for Gracie, and with her mother's permission would be back to build an overhead rope tether so she could have freedom of movement in the unfenced backyard.

The guys returned a few days later with the promised tether, which G had engineered, and even cleaned up the debris-filled yard so Gracie would not hurt herself now that she had more room to move around the yard.

As Rescue Ink pulled away from the house after that second visit, Johnny noted with satisfaction that Gracie was comfortably peering out of her new digs, finally protected from the elements. Even though she was still relegated to the backyard and tied up twenty-four hours a day, not the best life for a dog, it was the best life Gracie could hope to have for now.

Pit bulls like Gracie are the Tribbles of the dog world; they just keep multiplying with no end in sight.

In almost every municipal shelter in the New York metropolitan area—and in many cities around the country—pit bulls have taken the place of the shepherd mix as the ubiquitous dog in the chain-link kennel run. Some American pit bull terriers are bred by legitimate breeders who enter them in competitive events such as weight-pulling, or who place them with responsible owners who train them as therapy and obedience dogs. But the vast majority of pit bulls come from backyard breeders—casual and often uninformed owners who think they can make a mint from selling a tough-looking dog with a reputation to match.

Perhaps the pit bull's greatest tragedy is how dramatically its reputation has plummeted in the last century. Once the quintessential American frontier dog, the pit bull was the protector of home and hearth and gentle guardian of children. During World War I, pit bulls were depicted on war posters, symbols of perseverance and patriotism. Helen Keller owned one. So did Thomas Edison, Woodrow Wilson, and Fred Astaire. As role models go, devoted Petey of *The Little Rascals* was the Platonic ideal of any dog for much of the twentieth century.

But breeds can be ruined in what seems like a heartbeat when they attract the wrong owners for the wrong reasons. Pit bulls' heavily muscled bodies, strong jaws, and wide heads give them a generally tough look, which is often accentuated by cropping, or cutting, their ears. Perceived as an accessory that instantly confers machismo, pit bulls have suffered the worst case of character assassination of any breed. Once they became the favorites of street thugs and gangsters, some of these loyal dogs were fashioned into living weapons, a transformation abetted by their own hardwired desire to please their master, no matter how heartless or bloodthirsty.

Ironically, in the old-fashioned fighting pits that gave the breed its name, aggression against humans in the dogs was simply not tolerated. A fighting dog that bit a human, even in the heat of battle, did not live to fight another day, and was dispatched with a bullet to the head. Today's two-bit dog-fighters enthusiastically breed dogs for an edginess toward humans, though most pit bulls stubbornly retain their genetically entrenched love of people.

Pit bull public relations has reached such a low point that legislators have simply begun to outlaw these dogs, though no one can truly agree on the definition of a pit bull. Confounding matters is the fact that the American pit bull terrier, as the breed is formally called, is very elastic and nonstandardized in build and size. And other breeds are frequently confused with it, including the American Staffordshire terrier (the pit bull's AKC-recognized counterpart) and the Staffordshire bull terrier, which is another breed entirely. Pit bulls, or any dog thought to be a pit bull, are illegal in major cities from Denver to Toronto today. Breed-specific legislation, or BSL, assumes dogs will behave a certain way based on their breed, without factoring in their training, breeding, or socialization. "Punish the deed, not the breed" is the anti-BSL slogan, though stereotypes of child-chomping pits often obscure the logic of that argument.

Because of pit bulls' undeservedly bad reputation, adoptive homes are frequently few and far between. There is only one fate worse than meeting the needle at a municipal shelter: Being used as "bait" by a dogfighter who wants to teach his canine protégé to love the taste of blood is a terrible, though brief, existence for a dog.

Of course Johnny O can't say for sure, but he thinks this is the likely fate that awaited his Lucy before he rescued her. Lucy is now as much a constant in his life as his Clark Kent glasses or the small hoop earrings he wears in some of his seven ear piercings. "Animals have always come into my life," Johnny explains, among them two rescued bearded dragons that his kids named Phil and Lil. Today, a decade later, he still uses tweezers to feed the reptiles strawberry slices, and they ride on his shoulder when he vacuums. "But ever since I was a teenager, I've always wanted a pit bull."

For years, obstacles thwarted that dream—an erratic schedule, frequent traveling, then, once he was married, young children. So to get his fix of these broad-headed, rip-muscled canines, six-foot-two Johnny went to local shelters to walk them and teach them basic commands, "just to familiarize myself with them a little more."

Lucy wandered into Johnny's life independently of Rescue Ink. She had been born in a run-down house in Queens. A local rescue group had been keeping an eye on the house and the puppies, worried that the pups might be headed for the fighting pit. They tried twice to approach the residents and remove the puppies, which were almost six months old by the time they made their last attempt. On their third visit, they found the house abandoned and the littermates wandering nearby on the side of the Long Island Expressway, a six-lane highway that bisects the island into north and south.

Johnny adopted Lucy from the rescue group, and she has been a model canine ever since. With a blaze of white fur down her foreface and a dollop at the tip of her tail, she catches the eyes of total strangers, who stop Johnny in the street to pet her. At home, Lucy greets guests joyfully, washes their faces with her lapping tongue, and looks up with half adoration, half attentive concern whenever Johnny speaks.

Her mild manners would have made her well suited to be a bait dog, as would her gender, says Johnny. Females are desirable because they prompt males to compete and become even more aggressive. And if they are light colored, white especially, so much the better, as the blood shows up starkly against their fur, a visual reminder of the objective of the fight for the dogs being trained for such hair-trigger brutality.

"My goal as a rescue guy is I really want to educate people on pit bulls, because I really believe that people's perception of them could change," Johnny says. "It's not bad dogs, it's bad owners. As basic as that is, and as much as people have heard it a hundred times, the truth is the truth." The dogs are not to blame.

Like many of Rescue Ink's members, Johnny O's personal story is a contrast between the turbulence and even violence of his early years, and a tenderness and appreciation for animals that was always present but flourished as he grew older and wiser.

Johnny grew up in Levittown, the former expanse of Long Island potato fields that was converted into slab-house lots for returning World War II veterans in the late 1940s and early 1950s. Its cookie-cutter houses soon became an icon of modern suburbia. The youngest of four, Johnny, now forty-four, was raised by two teachers. His father encouraged a deep love of sports, and his mother, a trained opera singer and dancer, required each of her children to play an instrument. Johnny chose the drums. From elementary through high school, he pursued dance training in order to cement the coordination he needed for martial arts and sports like baseball and basketball. He especially liked jazz numbers—"explosive things," he explains.

Despite those extracurricular activities, the young Johnny always seemed to find trouble. He tried his first cigarette at seven, started smoking in earnest at twelve, and inevitably followed tobacco with stronger stuff. He went to a Catholic high school where, instead of more discipline, he encountered a socioeconomic diversity that allowed drugs to flourish: kids from the richer neighborhoods had more money to get themselves and their friends high.

There are things Johnny did when he was high and bored that he's not exactly proud of. "I was the typically quiet kid, but very volatile underneath," Johnny says of his high school days, when he hung out with both the jocks and the burnouts. "And at that age, when you're that young, you don't have control in terms of anger."

After high school, Johnny went to hotel-management school with the hope of becoming a chef, but he walked away after a year when a modeling opportunity presented itself. Though today his head is totally shaved, back then he had curly brown hair and "that Roman look," he explains. He also started personal training part-time. In between the print and runway work, he did stints as a doorman and bouncer at Long Island's many nightspots.

It was as a bouncer that he saw firsthand the power of emotions and how he could change them using just his own body language. "When someone's angry, you have to approach them with the opposite of what they're feeling," Johnny says. "That's why I wear glasses, and I walk up with my hands in my pockets, and say, real quiet and relaxed, 'Just give me five minutes of your time.'" Most of the time, that defused the situation. Patrons who didn't heed the "calming signals" he was sending soon found themselves surrounded by a phalanx of bouncers, and headed for the door. "It's called reflection—how you reflect off a mirror," says Johnny about how people instinctively emulate the emotional cues of another. "It's a very delicate but important word."

And that, he says, is what's so telling about animals: how they, too, mirror back what humans feel. Johnny's steady gaze and noncommittal expression are difficult to read, but Lucy is a predicable barometer. When Johnny is relaxed and calm, she is goofily gregarious and good-natured; when he is preoccupied, she is on edge and easy to startle.

"I can relate to them," says Johnny of the pit bull breed. "They are strong, and loyal. And stubborn."

While pits like Lucy and Gracie are far and away Johnny's favorites, no species has exclusivity when it comes to rescue, including that old cliché, the cat in the tree.

In the middle of a hot Long Island summer in June 2008,

Rescue Ink received a call about a male cat that had been up a tree in the South Shore town of Seaford for three days. A contractor had opened a door at the cat's house and accidentally let him slip out.

"He was up a big oak tree in someone's backyard, and I was told that if there was a ladder leaning against the tree when I got there, that meant he was still up there," says Johnny, who lives a half-dozen towns away from Seaford. "I'm not a cat person," he says matter-of-factly, "but I'll rescue them."

When Johnny pulled up to the house, there was the tree, and there was the ladder. And there, about sixty feet overhead, was a gray kitty with black stripes. With a sigh, Johnny started climbing the twenty-five-foot ladder. When he ran out of rungs, he continued climbing the branches. As he advanced, the cat retreated, climbing still higher. After about fifty feet, with the cat still retreating, Johnny reluctantly climbed down.

By now, a small crowd had gathered. "That's one of the guys from Rescue Ink," one neighbor was heard whispering. A veterinarian whose office was down the block ambled over to offer a free exam if the cat ever returned to earth.

Johnny tried everything to coerce that stubborn cat to return to terra firma. He moved the ladder and tried climbing from another vantage point. He called the local volunteer fire department, which begged off, saying feline rescue was not in its purview.

Johnny doesn't get frustrated easily, and this cat had yet to make a dent in his usual Zen approach. But he knew a storm was due to arrive the next day, and he was worried the cat wouldn't make it through. Three hours in, Johnny called a tree service. The owner arrived, looking spiffy in his dress khakis and golf shirt—he had already changed into his "off hours" clothes. He peered up into the leafy expanse. "He said, 'We're closed for the day, and I'd normally charge $550, but I'll do it for $335,'" remembers Johnny, who handed him a Rescue Ink card. "All right," reconsidered the tree pro after glancing at the card. "I'll do it for nothing. I'll be back in a half hour."

Johnny wasn't sure whether the guy would return, but he organized the assembled crowd anyway. Gathering up pool covers, blankets, and tarps, the neighbors positioned themselves in the four adjacent backyards, covering any ground where a feline in free fall might possibly land.

True to his word, the arborist returned with a cherry picker. He raised himself in the boom lift's bucket until he reached the vicinity of the marooned kitty and then optimistically extended a net with an open can of tuna fish inside. The cat was unimpressed. There was no choice but to cut the tree limb with the cat still on it.

The roar of a chain saw filled the air, a cloud of sawdust billowed earthward, and then the oak branch acceded to gravity and plummeted, soon losing its feline squatter. The cat bounced off one of the waiting pool covers, and immediately ran under a nearby shed. An onlooker with some potent-smelling catnip eventually lured him out.

Finally, seven hours after Johnny O arrived (and after three days of hugging the tree), the delinquent cat was home.

A gym rat since he was a teenager, Johnny worked for twenty-five years as a personal trainer. His athletic abilities come in handy not just for cat climbing, but also for duck diving.

A month after the cat caper, Rescue Ink received another phone tip, this time about an injured duck that had hurt its wing and been separated from its flock at a condominium development in the Suffolk County town of Smithtown.

Most of the Rescue Ink guys own pit bulls, pit mixes, or bully breeds, including Joe, Ant, Batso, and G. And while ducks are hardly their specialty, they responded to this call, perhaps as much to assuage the surrounding homeowners' concerns as to save the imperiled duck, who as yet didn't seem too concerned.

It goes without saying that the Rescue Ink guys are big. But most of them are also bulky, which means that acrobatic moves are not in most of their repertoires.

"If there's climbing involved, they know I'm a monkey," says Johnny, who jumped over an iron-topped fence and then down a retaining wall to reach the feathered focus of his efforts. "I didn't even think, I just did it."

It was raining hard that day, and the water in the walled-off area where the duck had ended up reached the middle of Johnny's calves. Johnny had a wire cage and net. The duck had an escape plan; he waddled through a wide pipe. Johnny slogged through the mud and sludge into the pipe after him, emerging on the other side of the tunnel.

The Boy Scouts' motto is: Be prepared. Rescue Ink's motto is: Figure something out fast.

Johnny had a net and a crate, but the guys ten feet above him had no way to help him or the duck to get out. Bruce noticed a mason had been working on a nearby footbridge across one of the ponds, and borrowed a broomstick and ladder. Johnny netted the duck, but the bird's head found a hole in the netting, and he started pecking. Johnny held the duck's beak shut, delicately pushed his head back into the net, and opened the crate. Gently, he dropped the flustered bird inside.

Big Ant reached in with the borrowed broomstick and lifted the crate out.

"Big guys, little duck," Johnny reflects, adding that no other rescue group responded to neighbors' calls about the stranded duck. "If you take away the macho crap for a minute, these are God's creatures. And it felt good getting that duck out."

Getting Johnny out was a little more difficult. The guys above extended the ladder horizontally, and Johnny shimmied across the pond on it from the retaining wall while G and Ant held it steady.

The woman who had called Rescue Ink took the newly freed duck home, washed the mud and slime off it, and then reunited it with its flock. And Rescue Ink went off to return their borrowed rescue gear.

Poised and punctual, Johnny is a man who's in control. He gets up at four thirty most mornings, a leftover habit from his many years as a personal trainer, when he had to get to clients' homes before they boarded their commuter trains and began their workdays. While Johnny is very much in control, you also get a sense that there is so very much under the surface for him to be in control of.

A partier and drinker until his early twenties, Johnny imbibes nothing but water, green tea, or juice today. He stopped because, quite frankly, he was enjoying it too much, and he'd had a couple of close calls—car accidents and a few mornings when he didn't remember how he got home. He fell off the wagon twice before making the decision to stay clean and sober. "Now I don't even take Advil unless I'm dying," he says.

Johnny has been trained in Tracy's Kenpo, a close-in style of martial arts fighting that taught him "how to break someone's neck, or how to stab them using your hand like the blade of a knife, or how to pull eyes from the socket." He knows he is capable of great violence, but he chooses control and discipline instead.

Johnny runs his hand over the tattoo that covers most of his right arm. The proper term for this kind of artwork in tattoo-parlor parlance is a sleeve. It depicts some of the animals held sacred in Chinese culture, a nod to the Eastern influence of his martial-arts training. On his inner bicep is the crane, symbolizing longevity and, as for many birds in many cultures, a conduit to the afterlife. The tiger, ferocious and deadly, always ready to pounce and ward off harm, slinks above his elbow. The snake, mysterious and stealthy, is right below, wrapping around his forearm. And above them all, extending down from his upper arm, is the dragon, his fiery breath communicating authority and mastery. The tattoos "are a story," he explains. "My life story." As such, they are never quite complete. The ink on his left arm portrays an allegory of life and death. His grandmother, depicted as an angel, is cupped in divine hands surrounded by ivy and chains. A man and woman are intertwined, their features blurred intentionally because they represent an ideal, not individuals.

While most of the Rescue Ink guys are married, Johnny O is not, though he was once. His son and daughter were two and five when he became a single dad. Owning a home on the same Levittown block where he grew up, he had his children dressed and ready for the school bus first thing in the morning, then left for the gym to train his clients. Doing freelance work as a "personal security specialist"—read "bodyguard"—late at night meant that he was home in the evenings for home-work, dance recitals, and sports games.

"Everything stopped," he says of becoming a father in his mid-twenties. "People say it ruined my 'thing,'" which included playing the drums in a rock band. "But everything's a new chapter. It's a healthy thing for change to happen."

The news about Gracie came roughly six months after Rescue Ink dropped off her doghouse. The person who made the original phone call to Rescue Ink about Gracie was supposed to be keeping tabs on her. But then Bruce got a tip from a different source that a dog fitting Gracie's description was at a local kill shelter. Johnny went to check it out.

Sure enough, it was the feminine little pit bull that he remembered. But she was no longer outgoing and playful. Now she cringed at his touch and looked around panic-stricken for a place to run.

"I'd have been scared, too," commiserated Johnny about Gracie's reaction to the world outside her backyard. He made arrangements with the shelter for Rescue Ink to take Gracie after she had been spayed, something the original owner never did take care of.

Sad to say, many of the pit bulls in whose lives Rescue Ink intervenes will never have the life that Lucy has, lounging on the couch all day and running at dawn on the beach. Some of them will live in barrels turned on their sides, heavy chains around their necks to "toughen them up." And while it bothered Johnny that the confident Gracie he knew half a year ago had changed into this frightened, skittish soul, he also knew that Gracie had a shot at a happy ending, because being a neglected or abused pit bull is not destiny. The Michael Vick dogs proved that.

In 2007, revelations that Atlanta Falcons quarterback Michael Vick was involved in breeding and training fighting dogs brought this underground world to television sets and newspaper pages around the world. At its most sophisticated levels, dogfighting is meticulously organized, with wagers in the six figures and security tight as a drum. The Vick dogs were part of this more "elite" fighting society. His Bad Newz Kennels was focused on wins, and the ruthless culling of any dog that did not measure up—by electrocution, drowning, strangulation, or even sheer blunt force—spoke powerfully to how serious they were.

By contrast, most of the "fighting" dogs that Rescue Ink comes across are at the bottom of the dogfighting pyramid: Sold for a couple of hundred dollars at most, they are raised in low-income neighborhoods where the fights are usually spontaneous, the organizers bored teenagers, and the only prize is bragging rights. In the street, among these pit owners, the negative media coverage of Bad Newz Kennels had the opposite effect: No matter what public criticism or jail time was meted out to their famous owner, the Vick dogs only glorified the sport among the most down-and-out. After all, not everyone has access to an NFL career. But most everyone has access to a dog.

In defiance of the conventional wisdom, the Vick dogs are not only surviving; many are thriving. One is enrolled in a children's reading program. Three others, with several more in training, are therapy dogs who visit cancer patients and troubled teenagers. And at least a half dozen have passed the American Kennel Club's Canine Good Citizen (CGC) test, a course in basic canine manners. They prove that one thing that is infinitely more powerful than the pit bull's imposing physique is its capacity to forgive.

When it came time to pick up Gracie at the municipal shelter, all the Rescue Ink guys went along for the ride. She was just going down the road, to a no-kill facility called Little Shelter, but it was miles away in terms of her prospects. At Little Shelter, there would be no threat of her being euthanized to make space for new arrivals. There she'd have the best chance at a new start, a brighter future than the one Johnny glimpsed for her when he left her earlier that year with owners who never took to heart Rescue Ink's advice or help.

Johnny walked Gracie out of the shelter on a thick rope lead, then knelt down to pet her. She jumped up on him, flinging her front paws around his neck, a sign of insecurity. In Gracie's scary new world, the only safe thing, it seemed, was Johnny. "Rescue to me is just a small piece of the puzzle," he says, noting with satisfaction that Gracie had a roomy cage and plush bed at Little Shelter. "It's an epidemic. When we're so busy rescuing, that's a bad sign because that means there are a lot of problems out there. It's kind of frightening to think there are that many people that neglect animals and think nothing of it."

With the addition of Lucy to his life, his dream of having a pit bull of his own finally realized, Johnny's thinking of getting some more tattoo work done. His tattoo artist, Ray Alfano, has a waiting list—animal portraits are his specialty—but Johnny thinks he can squeeze him in. All Johnny needs is a really good picture of Lucy, maybe a three-quarter profile, to show off her dark, gentle eyes. He's not sure where the tattoo will go yet—on his calf, maybe, or his back. Regardless of location, that tattoo will stand not only for the first pit bull to share his life and his home, but also for all the other rescued pits, some who have become success stories, some who met tragic and fatal ends, and some for whom no ending is known. It will stand for all the dogs who have become part of his story, not to mention all the ones he has yet to meet.

Say good night, Gracie.

3

Eric

La Dolce Vita

What good is a guard dog if his eyes are glued shut with pus and he's too emaciated to stand without wobbling?

The Rescue Ink guys stood in a bitterly cold backyard in Bellport, on Long Island's South Shore, contemplating this question. It was a big group that had responded to a tip about two dogs who were outside day in and day out with inadequate shelter: Eric, Johnny O, Big Ant, Angel, and G, as well as Robert and Bruce. In front of them were two plywood doghouses so poorly made that even the slightest gust of wind whistled through them. Chained to each flimsy shelter was a dog. On the left, a young pit bull strained against his short chain. And on the right, a Rottweiler named Nike who was so thin his hip bones protruded, and who had eyes so infected it looked like they had been smeared with custard, sat glumly, unaware of his large audience.

The guys had come to talk to the owner about bringing by new doghouses, or at least weatherproofing the old ones. But the owner, who had answered the door with a mixture of indifference and relief, had a different idea. "Personally I'd like to see both dogs go," the owner said. He was unemployed and on dialysis. He had left the dogs' care to his nieces and nephews, who were unreliable at best. "I'm not capable of keeping them," he said of the dogs. "I'm hardly capable of taking care of myself."

As his owner approached him, Nike wagged his body and lowered himself deferentially—not easy, since he could barely stand on his weak rear legs. A length of wooden two-by-four sat near his house; the kids used it to push the food bowl to Nike, the man explained. They preferred to interact with the pit bull, who was younger and cuter. (And not blinded by gross pus.)

The man could not remember how old the Rottweiler was. He was old, he insisted. It felt like he'd had him forever. Fifteen years, maybe sixteen even.

Eric inched himself closer to Nike and put his hand on his massive head. The black-and-rust-colored dog leaned against him.

The guys reached a consensus almost without talking: It was clear that the two dogs could not stay here another day. Nike and the pit bull were loaded into the waiting Rescue Ink van. The owner looked on dispassionately, as if watching old appliances being taken away. Nike rode in a wire crate in back; the pit perched contentedly on Johnny O's lap.

Everyone was worried about Nike, especially Eric. It was amazing that the dog had survived as long as he had. Sick as he was and presumed to be elderly, if not as ancient as the owner claimed, with a couple more 19-degree days like this one in December of 2008, Nike would have never made it to spring.

"Of course I'm angry at the person who was doing this to

this dog, but I've gotta turn it into a positive," Eric said as he got back into the van for the ride to Save-a-Pet in Port Jefferson, where a vet was standing by to see Nike. "I could be pissed off at this guy, or I could be happy that he surrendered the dogs to us."

There was one more person Eric was angry at, and that was himself. Because he lived relatively close by, he had originally volunteered to check out the address. And Eric had driven by, noted the heavy chains on the dogs and the inadequate housing. It was a bad situation, but it didn't look like an emergency, and the guys try not to go into potentially dangerous situations without backup unless the animal is at risk.

Eric had not noticed how dire the Rottie's condition was because the dog had been in the farthest corner of the yard, away from the street. Had Eric known, he wouldn't have waited another day or two for Rescue Ink to assemble. He would have banged on the door alone, dealt with it then and there. He'd done it before, and would do it again. He just wished he had known.

Eric Olsen, thirty-three, is the newest member of Rescue Ink, and perhaps one of the most physically imposing. He has piercing blue eyes and a voice as rough as sandpaper. On his right arm is a tattoo of a snarling Rottweiler that seems ready to leap off his skin.

Eric's first dog was Marley, a Rottie mix he adopted as a puppy from North Shore Animal League. Next came the miniature pinschers, sort of like crosses between Dobermans and mosquitoes: Axle, the self-appointed leader, who steadfastly refuses to give kisses; Diesel, adopted from a guy Eric worked with as a nightclub bouncer who was severely allergic to the pint-size canine; and Kash, the smallest and most laid-back of the trio. Finally, there is Chloe, a Chihuahua mix whom his wife Jennifer acquired before they met.

"I have small dogs, it doesn't bother me," says Eric about his little ones. "I pick them up and kiss them and hold them—it's no big deal. I don't care that my dog's fifteen pounds. I don't need a pit bull or a Rottweiler to walk down the street and act tough. That's not being tough. That's just like wearing a big necklace to make you look tough. Take all that away, and you are what you are."

There used to be a sixth dog in Eric's pack, a young female Rottweiler. She is not the dog depicted in Eric's tattoo, but she is the dog that inspired it, his blanket statement about his love for the breed. One day Eric saw her in a pet store, her nose buried in the corner of the cage. Upset to see the growing puppy in the small, dirty enclosure, he kept returning. Finally, though he knew he shouldn't—giving even a dollar to a pet store that sells puppies supports the puppy millers who supply them—he offered the pet store $300 instead of the $1,200 they were asking, and the puppy was his.

Eric named her Dolce, the Italian word for "sweet," and for a while she lived up to her name. She was a fast learner, eagerly picking up the commands he taught her.

But as she entered doggie adolescence around eighteen months of age, Dolce was also quick to take offense at the slightest provocation from the original lady of the house, Marley. Now eight, Marley had Addison's disease, and was grumpy with the new arrival. But to Dolce, a growl was nothing short of a declaration of war. Once the dogfights between Dolce and Marley started, they escalated at a frightening pace. The two couldn't even be in a room together because Eric could never predict what would spark a conflict.

Eric remembers their last fight vividly. Facing off in the backyard, each dog alternated taking a death grip on the neck of the other. Eric raced outside and tried everything to break them apart. He pulled them by their rear legs, doused them with the hose, even tried hitting them with a nearby two-by-four.

"My wife came out with a leash, and I stuck the hose down one of the dogs' throat. Finally, I got them separated," Eric says. "I was covered in blood, saturated." Marley was riddled with puncture wounds. And Dolce's neck look like ground hamburger meat.

Realizing that he would never be able to trust the two together, Eric confined Dolce to a spare room. He brought a television in to keep her company and slept beside her every night. Slowly, he acceded to the reality that was as hard as the floor beneath him: These two dogs were locked in a battle to the death. Neither would be dissuaded, even by him. Someone would have to lose. And it would probably be Marley.

Eric met Rescue Ink thanks to Axle, his hyperactive miniature pinscher. Always thinking, Axle is able to execute, with military precision, kitchen raids by pulling the blanket through his crate and using it to drag the wire cage to the counter. Then he hops on to see what goodies have been left out for him to sample. Eric decided that agility, a timed competition in which dogs navigate an obstacle course with their handlers, would be a great way to channel Axle's energy. At an outdoor agility class in the summer of 2008, where obsessively focused border collies scrambled over A-frames and sailed over jumps, Eric ran into someone who noticed his tattoos and mentioned a new rescue group called Rescue Ink. They would be at a fund-raising event called Hounds on the Sound in a couple of weeks.

Eric was only half listening: He had heard "tattoos," and thought perhaps these guys were tattoo artists with a soft spot for animals. "My tattoo guy had moved to Florida," he says, so he went to the charity event looking for a replacement artist. Instead, he met the guys, learned they were about rescues first and tattoos second, and left with an invitation to join the group at some future events.

Rescue Ink doesn't close ranks around a new member very easily, but Eric was a natural fit for this group. With his burly build and tattoos, he not only looked the part, but his single-minded focus on animals spoke volumes.

Because Eric lives farther east on Long Island than anyone else in the group, he was conveniently located to check out complaints and suspected abuse cases on the eastern end of the island, as he had with Nike the Rottweiler. His first case was a guy who kept his pit bull outdoors in a crate, all day and all night, during the summer. The only thing protecting the eight-month-old tan-and-white female from the sun and rain was a flimsy sheet of plastic covering the top.

"Why do you have her if you keep her locked up all the time?" Eric asked the owner.

"So I can make money off her puppies," came the brusque, if honest, reply.

Eric sighed. Even if he managed to talk the guy into giving up the sweet female pit bull, the guy would just get another. This was a situation where he would have to abandon the best-case scenario, and just settle for the better-than-worst-case one.

"I had a dog house that I had bought and painted for Dolce, so I gave it to him," Eric says.

He had already come to the decision, as much as it pained him, that he would need to find Dolce a new home. When—not if, but when—there was another fight, Marley would never survive. Because Dolce was younger and purebred, she was a better adoption prospect. So Eric got to work, contacting rescue groups about leads for placing Dolce.

When Eric posted his problem with Dolce on various online chat groups for Rottweiler owners, he got more flak than support. "You're not trying hard enough," the cyber-experts chided him. It didn't matter to them that Eric planned to keep Dolce until he found her the perfect home. They saw no shades of gray—only black and white.

Eric understood that it wasn't a stark matter of right or wrong, but rather a need to make the best out of a bad situation. Animal advocates often take a similarly hard line about dogs living outside. "An outdoor dog has an address, but not a home," is one commonly heard refrain. And it's true that many outdoor dogs lack the socialization of their indoor counterparts. Often isolated and ignored, they do not feel like a member of their family's "pack," and are denied this important social interaction, which gives them a sense of security and belonging.

But the reality is that not all cultures accept the idea of dogs in the home. Rescue Ink isn't in the business of making things absolutely perfect for every animal that comes its way: That just isn't feasible. The only thing the guys can hope to do is to leave things a little better than when they first found them.

Consider the case of Renee's dogs. She called Rescue Ink with a problem: She had a male Rottweiler and a female mastiff–Great Dane mix who were simply too big for her small West Hempstead house. She couldn't afford a doghouse, so in good weather she tied them to a tree in the side yard. They ran around the tree, creating a dust bowl, and dug holes the size of moon craters. Feces filled the yard.

Renee was also reluctant to spay the female Dane mix, or neuter the male Rottweiler. It wasn't a matter of money—Rescue Ink had offered to pay for the operations—she just kept hedging and saying her dogs weren't ready yet. Amazingly, the two dogs had never had puppies, which Renee had attributed to the fact that the Rottweiler wasn't tall enough to reach his mark. Nonetheless, the guys stressed to Renee how important it was for both dogs to be fixed, especially if the female was going to be outside, a target for any male that wandered by.

"One step at a time," said Big Ant about Renee's reluctance to spay and neuter her dogs. "We're going to build her an enclosure, and then we'll talk about the next step with her." Rescue Ink knows that it's often up against stubbornly held beliefs.

The guys volunteered to build Renee a doghouse, a promise that turned out to be the rescue equivalent of a barn raising. These dogs were *big*, and needed a house roomy enough to accommodate both of them.

With $600 worth of supplies donated by a local lumber company, the guys spent an entire day building the design they had sketched out. The roof, which reached their chests, was sloped to shed the rain and finished off with real roofing tiles. The sides were made of two sheets of plywood with insulation in between. After a coat of off-white paint, Big Ant applied Rescue Ink stickers to the front and side. This wasn't a doghouse; it was a condo.

"Doghouses are very expensive," Eric notes. "If you were

to buy this one, they would probably charge you anywhere from two to three thousand dollars"—not something Renee was going to be able to budget for anytime soon.

Borrowing a forklift, the guys loaded the doghouse onto a trailer, then towed it to Renee's house. With a lot of maneuvering on her narrow street, they positioned the doghouse at the far end of her backyard, up against the six-foot fence bordering the neighbors, where it would be as protected from the elements as possible.

Along with the rest of the guys, Eric stepped back to survey their handiwork. Once the weather thawed a bit, they'd send a contractor over to put a permanent chain-link fence around the enclosure.

"I'd rather the dogs be inside the house, but if they can't, this is the next best thing," said Eric as the two dogs sniffed their new home away from home. "This is probably better insulated than my house. So I think they'll be all right."

It was painful to watch Nike slowly make his way up the ramp to the examination room at Save-a-Pet.

"It kills me," said Eric. "I can see that the dog is just tired"—tired of the unrelenting hunger and cold, tired of being sick and in pain.

Inside, veterinarian Kenneth Palladino of the Veterinary Medical Center in Central Islip gave Nike a gentle once-over. Though his heart and lungs sounded good, Nike was obviously malnourished and dehydrated. His uncooperative rear legs, which frequently fell out from under him, were likely a result of muscle wasting and poor nutrition. He wasn't even that old—maybe four or five.

"His teeth are pretty bad, and really worn down," Dr. Palladino said. "It looks like he's been chewing rocks and sticks," probably because there was no other entertainment or diversion in the backyard where he was chained.

The prescription for Nike was straightforward enough: He needed to go on antibiotics to deal with not just the eye infections but also deep ear infections that were likely causing him much discomfort. Small, frequent meals would help him add to his body mass and gain strength.

And he was going to need it: A blood test revealed that Nike had heartworm, a debilitating disease that can easily be prevented with regular screening and a monthly preventive pill. The cure for heartworm used to contain arsenic, and dogs often died of the treatment. Today, the medication is not as toxic, but it still puts a strain on the body. But Nike had months of healing ahead of him before he would be strong enough to undergo the expensive heartworm treatments.

Within hours, Nike's life had changed dramatically—and for the better. And that was only because someone in his neighborhood had taken the time to report his neglect to Rescue Ink. "What people have to realize is, all you gotta do is make one call, that's it," Eric says. "You don't have to say who you are, nothing. That one person who called just saved a dog's life."

Knowing that someone is watching is often enough to make people do the right thing, to jog their conscience and make them start taking care of their animals like the sentient beings they are, not the objects they're being treated as.

One summer morning in 2008, Eric saw a Rottweiler locked in a crate in a garage. It was 90 degrees out, and the garage was obviously not air-conditioned.

When he came home after a full day of mowing lawns and

trimming Bartlett pear trees, Eric noticed that nothing about the dog's situation had changed: He was still in the crate in the sweltering heat.

Eric called Johnny O, and the two went over to explain to the owner that the Rottie couldn't even stand up in the tight crate. He needed more room to move around. The owner agreed to try to bring him into the house more often, even though his brother, who lived with him, was scared of dogs.

Eric went back on his own a few days later to offer the man a chain-link pen for his dog, but the guy wasn't home, and though he left his number, he never got a call back.

Then, a few months after that, about a month before Eric met Nike, he passed by this other Rottweiler's house yet again, and saw the dog in a crate outside. It was raining and sleeting, but the dog stayed out there exposed to the elements for three hours. A sympathetic neighbor let Eric take pictures from his property to document the neglect.

But he never needed to use them. Later that night, Rescue Ink hurriedly built a doghouse and dropped it off at the house. Eric has yet to see the dog use it—and that's not a bad thing. "After I saw that dog out in the rain I went by and told the guy, 'I pass here every single day, and I'm going to be watching,'" Eric remembers. The anger in his voice must have reached its mark: "The dog's inside now," he says with satisfaction. It's one case, at least, where he managed to effect the best-case scenario. And when those experiences come along, he relishes them—they are so often so few and far between.

A shelter staffer took Nike's rope lead and led him to the steel cage where he would be convalescing. As soon as she opened it, he rushed inside, looking around as if incredulous at his good fortune.

"At least this dog will be warm tonight," said Eric as the Rescue Ink van rolled away.

Eric visited Nike every couple of weeks after his rescue. The first time, Nike was a bit steadier on his feet, but he did not like anyone touching his head, likely because of the ear infections. "The vet techs said he was a little touchy, but I just opened the cage and gave him a treat," Eric says. He walked Nike around the shelter for a bit; it was too cold to go outside. "After about twenty minutes he lay down, and I was able to rub his stomach. I was just massaging him, just letting him know that he's in a good place."

The next time, about a month after Nike had been taken in from the cold, Eric could see an appreciable difference in the handsome Rottie when he visited Save-a-Pet. His coat was shiny, and his eyes were entirely clear. He had put on a little weight—not enough, but some. Having lived so long in a backyard without any human contact, he was learning to trust the vet techs who worked with him daily, grooming him and teaching him basic manners.

"I couldn't believe how much weight he'd put on. He was actually walking, not sliding from his back hips. He had some muscle on his back legs," Eric remembers.

Eric loves all dogs, but he has a particular soft spot for Rottweilers, which he attributes to Dolce. Whenever he sees a neglected Rottie like Nike, it makes him want to see that dog end up in a good place, just as Dolce eventually did.

It was a six-and-a-half-hour drive from Long Island to southern Maine, where Dolce's new home awaited. Each mile that passed on the odometer was another heartache for Eric because he was that much closer to giving away his precious Rottie.

Eric had found Dolce's new owner, Ann, through a Maine-based Rottie rescue group. The minute he heard Ann's New England accent, he knew she and Dolce were a perfect match. "She sounded like a little old grandmother"—one who would have the time and attention to lavish on Dolce, and make the dog the center of her universe. They stayed on the phone for three hours—not typical for Eric, who's not much of a chitchatter.

Ann was in her late sixties, and had owned two Rottweilers. She didn't want her next dog to be a rambunctious puppy; she needed a well-trained, relatively calm dog. And because she had just dealt with the losses of her two elderly Rotties, she didn't want an older dog that didn't have much time left.

As soon as Eric pulled up to Ann's house, he knew he had made the right decision. "I saw a little Rottweiler garden flag. And then to the right, she had a little white picket fence with a nice garden where she buried her last Rottweiler, who she had told me about."

Ann watched as the tough guy opened the door to his car and, trying to hold back tears, walked Dolce to her front door. When he left, the scene replayed, wrenching her heart. She offered him money, but he waved her away. She was giving Dolce the life she wanted—as an only dog, the center of attention—and that was payment enough.

"Giving Dolce away was probably the hardest thing I've ever done," says Eric. "It hurt, and it took a long time to get over it."

Now, a year later, Ann still keeps in regular contact with Eric. She sends him cards and pictures of Dolce living a life of leisure—sleeping with Ann's fluffy gray-and-white cat, posing in front of a Victorian couch with her favorite toy, snuggling deep in a blanket during a power outage. He, in turn, sends packages of rawhides and stuffed animals, which Dolce digs into with gusto.

"She is such a gorgeous, beautiful dog," Ann says simply. "Eric brought Dolce here, and she is the love of my life. She is the best dog, and I think that is because of his training. He's the one who made her what she is."

In the summer, Ann and Dolce drive fifteen miles to the beach to have picnics on the pristine sand. Ann took a picture of Dolce on one of those jaunts with the local lighthouse in the background, which she put in a frame and sent to Eric. It's one of his prized possessions.

"I send letters as though Dolce is writing them," Ann says. "I still call him Dad." She shares details of Dolce's life: how she gleefully meets visitors at the door with an object, usually one of Ann's slippers or shoes. (Particularly beloved visitors are greeted with one of Dolce's precious stuffed teddy bears.) How she attends tea parties with Ann's four-year-old granddaughter, sitting politely amid the china and doilies. How she charms Ann's sister, who periodically expresses her distaste for dog and cat hair, by staring at her with her chocolate-brown eyes until she relents. "Yes, you are beautiful," Ann's sister will admit, giving Dolce a resigned pat.

Eric could not have ordered up a more storybook ending. "It was almost like I was meant to get this dog out of the pet store, train her right so I could pass her on to Ann," he says.

Maybe he believes in fate, maybe he doesn't. All he knows is his Dolce is loved, and that is all that matters.

On his last visit to the clinic, Eric again took Nike out of his crate and walked him outside. It was cold, but Nike was intent on exploring the shelter's tidy front yard. He peed on a few trees, watched the cars whoosh by, then gently took a large Milk-Bone from Eric's fingers and crunched away contentedly.

"The past is the past, and he's not thinking about it anymore," Eric muses. "He's thinking, 'I'm in a nice cozy cage right about now, food all of the time, I've got girls taking me out and walking me all day.' He's not living in the past, so we shouldn't."

Things would only get better for Nike: After he gained a bit more weight and strength, he would be neutered, which would only make him more obedient and easier to handle.

"He just reminds me of mine," says Eric of the Rottweiler he loved so much he gave her away. "And I just want to get him better."

4

Des

Cat Man Do

On a crystalline December day in 2008, the Rescue Ink van rattled along Montauk Highway.

Outside the black-tinted windows, the nondescript landscape of Suffolk County's south shore, liquor stores and autobody shops, pizzerias and vinyl-sided bars with neon signs, went by before it morphed into the fabulousness of the Hamptons.

The Rescue Ink guys had already been briefed on the case they were headed to: A middle-aged woman had been caring for a large group of cats in her house in the town of Center Moriches. Early on, more than a decade ago, there had been only a handful of cats, and while she had the occasional litter, she got most of the cats spayed and neutered. With the exception of one visiting tomcat with an interesting genetic mutation—extra toes, a harmless condition called polydactyly that made his offspring look like they were wearing snowshoes—she didn't bring many new cats into the mix.

Then, about a year ago, a financial crisis hit: With her

father's recent death, and the loss of his retirement income, she could no longer pay the bills and make ends meet. Surgeries to spay or neuter the cats went by the wayside, and her cat population mushroomed. Together with her chain-smoking octogenarian mother and her twenty-something son, she was being forced to leave the foreclosed house by April. And she knew that the cats could not come with her.

It was immediately assumed on the van ride over—and rightly so—that Des Calderon, Rescue Ink's resident cat guy, would take the lead on this case.

Nobody in Rescue Ink likes the word "expert." It's not because they don't have knowledge—they do. But when it comes to rescue, all the guys know it's a bad idea to brand themselves know-it-alls. Truth be told, even the most seasoned rescuer is always learning. When he starts to think he has seen it all, then he probably hasn't seen enough.

So, just as much as anyone, Des balks at the *E* word. "Experts don't make mistakes, and I want the freedom to be wrong, so I can learn and grow and improve what I do," he says. "When you're an expert, there's no margin for error." But as you watch Des transport a mewing calico by the scruff of her neck or check a kitten's gums to make sure they are not pale and dry, signaling dehydration, labels are meaningless anyway.

Des is something of an anomaly among his Rescue Ink colleagues. He's a cat lover in a pack of pit bull aficionados. Sure, several of the guys have cats, but none identifies so wholly and completely with these elegant, aloof, almost mystical creatures as Des does.

Des was in his usual biker uniform: leather jacket and skull rings. In truth, Des hasn't ridden since an accident three years ago, when he got hit by a pickup truck going forty miles an hour. Every piece of his bike was shattered, but somehow he walked away. Better not tempt fate, he thinks. (Or at least best to wait until his wife's memory of the accident fades a bit more.) But skull belt buckle aside, Des is apt to accessorize with flair. Today he has donned a pair of black rubber Crocs and camouflage pants.

Des's ever-present denim jacket with the sleeves cut off is as much a practicality as a fashion statement. The layered look satisfies Des's practical fetish for pockets. The vest and his cargo pants are crammed with tools of his cat-rescuing trade. There are rubber gloves, pens, a screwdriver, a flashlight, a box cutter. There are electrical ties, which he uses to fasten together the halves of plastic cat carriers. There's even an eye patch: When chasing wily cats who like to duck from bright sunlight into dark basements, Des just switches it from one eye to the other to instantly adjust his vision. He used to carry a stethoscope for locating cats hiding behind walls until someone stole it.

Usually Des gets a good-natured ribbing about some aspect of his apparel, but on this particular afternoon the interest centered on a gash above his left eyebrow. He shrugged off the questions, pulled his knit cap lower over his curly salt-and-pepper hair, and answered his ringing cell phone. Sifting through papers in his battered black briefcase, he settled into a serious-sounding conversation about a cat named Mittens and an ear-mite infestation.

No one else in Rescue Ink carries a briefcase. Des's is stuffed with vet records, deworming and vaccination schedules, phone numbers of dozens of rescuers, and a sheaf of spay and neuter appointments at the ASPCA outreach mobile clinic program in Manhattan.

A lifelong student of the power of words, Des chooses his methodically, holding forth eloquently on feral-cat overpopulation and management the way a poli-sci professor might lecture on federal economic policy. "It's very simple for me to see that the solution is widespread sterilization and then release back into their territory," he said. "You can't adopt them all because they are wild, and you can't euthanize them all."

There are about 850,000 feral cats in the metropolitan New York area, Des is often heard saying. That number is derived from a formula that estimates 0.5 cats for every household documented in the U.S. Census. And when well-intentioned residents feed these feral cats but do nothing to stop them from reproducing, they simply fuel the breeding-rate fire.

The house Rescue Ink was about to visit was a practical application of the mathematics of unneutered cat colonies: Like an algebraic equation on crack, a few unneutered cats can multiply into a population of many more digits.

Joe stopped the van with a lurch in front of a modest house with overgrown boxwood hedges. The vehicle's side doors flew open, and the guys spilled out—Angel, G, Johnny, and Eric. Joe took a final swig of his protein drink and slammed the driver's door shut. (Batso had been down for more than a week now with a bout of the flu.)

As soon as he stepped across the threshold and onto the stained, grimy parquet floor, Des knew that the son, who had called Rescue Ink for help, had not exaggerated the direness of the situation here. His mother stood in the dining room, obsessively spraying and scrubbing the worn wooden table with window cleaner. Around her, every vertical surface—the walls, the kitchen cabinets, the flat-panel TV in the corner—was coated with the urine spray of tomcats. The sofa cushions had long lost their fabric, their foam cores exposed and pock-marked with claw-carved indentations.

The acrid smell of urine and ammonia, with an undertone of decomposing cat shit, hung in the air with the weight of a thick fog. And still the woman sprayed and scrubbed.

"I spend all my time cleaning," she said. Six empty litter boxes were stacked on the kitchen table; an aluminum turkey pan filled with dry cat food sat in the middle of the living-room floor.

There's no doubt that a household of cats demands round-the-clock maintenance: Des once managed a shelter of eighty cats, and it was nearly a full-time job. "It would take three hours in the morning to feed and clean up after them," he says. "And at the end of the day, I had to repeat the process. And somewhere in between I had a full-time job."

Despite the woman's scrubbing, it was clear that she had long ago lost the hygiene battle with her tidal wave of cats. Her tidying assault on the table slowed as Des asked some questions in a nonjudgmental tone that, if it were characterized as a country, would undoubtedly be Switzerland.

"How many cats do you think you have?" he inquired softly.

"I don't know," she answered. "I stopped counting at a hundred and fifty."

Big Ant took a deep breath—an act of bravery in this stulti-fying house—but said nothing.

"I understand," Des nodded, writing in the notepad he always carries in one of his countless pockets. "Are they spayed and neutered?"

"Some," she continued. "But not the later ones . . . we just couldn't afford to take them to the vet. We can't even afford the ten dollars a day it takes to feed them."

"I know," he answered, sounding for all the world like he meant it, probably because he did. When it comes to cats and the people who love them, Des is respectful of the bond, even when it reaches a level most would call obsession.

Born in Colombia, South America, Des moved with his family to Jamaica—the Queens neighborhood, not the island—when he was nine. What both places had in common was an acceptance and even expectation that violence is an integral part of life, as inevitable as the sunrise.

Des remembers being beaten up by the kid across the street when he was a seven-year-old in Colombia. When he ran home crying to his grandmother, she refused to let him in. He needed to go back across the street and defend the family name, she said.

"I said to her, 'What should I do?'" Des remembers. "And she said, 'When it rains, you get an umbrella.'" Then she slammed the door in his face.

Left to figure out for himself what she meant, Des went over to a clump of bamboo, followed one of the thick stalks to the ground where it met the underground rhizome in a knob of black, peachlike fuzz, and broke it off. Then he went back across the street and returned the beating.

The beaten neighbor boy chased him home, but this time Des's grandmother opened the door to her grandson. Then, satisfied at seeing his bleeding opponent, she slammed the door again—this time in his pursuer's face.

Things were no better in the pothole-pocked streets of Jamaica, Queens, a predominantly poor black and Latino community that has been so for generations. "There were often knife fights after school," Des says. "You had two choices: You have your ass kicked, or you go around and kick ass."

So Des did the only logical thing: He joined a gang. It was a decision that helped him survive not just physically, but emotionally. Growing up in an abusive household, "the cool thing about a gang was it gave you a way to express yourself when you were angry," he explains. "Today they call it wilding. Back in my day we used to call it stomping. We'd wear steel-toed boots, put the guy on the floor, and stomp him. I found it exhilarating and exciting, and it made me laugh. It drew me in."

Ever the pragmatist, Des decided he might as well make a living wage off this violence. A voracious reader, he sought out an unlikely manual for learning how to effectively rob people: He borrowed a book on Carl Jung's theory of personality from the library.

"It was really hard. Every other page, I had to consult the dictionary. But I got through it," he says. And the Swiss psychologist's dissertations on how the collective unconscious and its enduring archetypes influence our behavior offered him practical tricks of the trade: Soft-spoken and baby-faced, Des was given the job of luring marks into a false sense of security so his colleagues could rob them. Some of their victims were Long Island commuters looking to score coke or marijuana. Others were pool hustlers heading home from a successful night of scamming.

"We didn't think of ourselves as criminals—we were ripping off people who wanted to buy drugs or were ripping other people off," Des says, noting how easily money comes spilling out of pockets once they are expertly torn off.

Back at the Center Moriches house, the woman finally stopped her scrubbing in response to Des's question about kittens. Yes, she had some. They were in a spare bedroom with their mothers.

In the small, unfurnished room down the hall, the kittens huddled around a collapsed metal bed frame covered in blankets. They were about five weeks old, not quite weaned, but old enough to be eating kitten food. Des crouched down and picked one up by the scruff. The little white cat with black spots had gooey-looking eyes and a green-crusted nose, signs, Des speculated, of an upper respiratory infection. Some of the kitten's siblings—or cousins, as parentage was a wild card at this point—looked equally affected. Judging from the foul-smelling, green-colored stools in the room, parasites such as coccidia or giardia were also a likelihood.

A crate was brought in from the van, and Des directed the guys to scoop up the ten or so kittens, along with one lactating adult female. They had already called ahead to a no-kill shelter, which would isolate the young ones and begin treatment. Because they were small and fluffy and precocious, their future was bright: Few adopters can resist the magnetic pull of a kitten.

Des also noticed a young female tortoiseshell who had a severely infected left eye. It was glazed over and shaded a dull blue. "We're going to take her, too, and get that eye looked at—she might lose it," he explained to the woman in that same measured and gentle tone, and she nodded in agreement.

Des's evolution into who he is today required an escape from his Queens neighborhood, which he likens to an isolated midwestern town. Though residents knew there was a big city just across the river, many never left, preferring instead to take their chances with the drug dealers at the corner bodega, because they were, in the end, less terrifying than the unknown land.

When Des got his first motorcycle at seventeen, he crossed the Queensboro Bridge into his future. Culture shock did not begin to cover it. Here in Manhattan there were women with strawberry blond hair and blue eyes. "The first time I heard somebody say, 'I'm a WASP,' I didn't know what that meant." He laughs. "Did she mean some kind of a bee?"

Des started studying Chinese kung fu at Alan Lee's Chinese Kung-Fu Wu-Su Association in Midtown. He had always been interested in dance, and this martial arts form's fluid moves were a close approximation. Des remembered a girl from his neighborhood who was an amazing dancer—"she wore these flowy white outfits, and looked like an angel." She had told him she had trained at the Phil Black Dance Studios, a popular jazz and tap school. Once he was transplanted to Manhattan, Des took classes there. After a while he began to teach and do choreography, eventually becoming Black's partner and successor. One of Des's students was a nineteen-year-old named Jennifer Lopez who was distracted by her college studies. Recognizing her star quality, he urged her to drop out to follow her muse.

Then one day almost a decade ago, Des faced a similar challenge to discard practicality for passion. In 2000, Des's wife, Molly, wanted a cat, and he obliged, albeit with some indifference. "I hated cats. I was a dog lover," Des says with a shrug. "What's the point of a cat? They're not affectionate. But that's because it's not my cat. I mean, your wife wouldn't jump on my lap. That's because she's your wife, not mine. Until you have your own cat, you really don't understand."

As innocuous as it seemed at the time, Kitty's arrival was a turning point for Des, an antidote to his routine of complacence. "I was working to pay the bills, then I'd come home, watch TV, and order Chinese food," he says. "I was just existing from day to day, with nothing to make my life meaningful." But now that Des had a cat at home, he delighted in just observing the physics of her stealthy, liquid movement.

He also began to notice the strays in lots and empty buildings in his Harlem neighborhood. "I assumed that they had always been there. But now I actually *saw* them." One weed-choked lot had a cardboard box filled with cute kittens. "Their eyes were swollen shut, and when I went to touch them, they ran away," he remembers. "I thought, 'Somebody should do something.'"

A passerby commented that the cats were feral. Des went home and looked up the unfamiliar word on the Internet. Once he understood that these cats had turned their backs on domesticity, he called every humane and animal-welfare agency he could think of to help with the kittens. Eventually, he realized, *he* was the somebody who needed to help with these cats.

Des got the ASPCA to agree to spay and neuter the cats if he trapped them, which he did. At first he focused on the friendlier, more adoptable cats and kittens. He found himself riding early-morning trains with cat carriers to get still more neighborhood cats fixed and vaccinated, then giving them to rescue groups to adopt out.

By 2004 he was a full-fledged cat advocate. When he wasn't working as a restaurant manager, he set up an outdoor stand for adoptions on the Upper West Side to find some of the tamer cats good homes. During the winter, Des bought a generator, and had a vent pumping hot air into his plastic-covered kitty crates. And in the summer, he used an air conditioner that pumped cool air into the crates.

A few months after Kitty became part of his life, Des was invested—and not just financially. Cat rescue gave him a sense of purpose, a connection to something larger. "It isn't just about working with that cat. It's about delivering something into people's lives that will bring joy to them," he says. "There's a surge of energy, and that makes you feel alive."

In the Center Moriches house, there were cats everywhere— on the back of the threadbare couch, in a urine-crusted carrier in the hallway, in an open-air enclosure accessed through the kitchen door. But the math did not add up to the 150-plus cats that the woman professed to own.

There are some in the basement, she admitted.

"Can we see them?" Des asked.

"No," the woman replied, avoiding eye contact. "It's a mess down there."

Des could see a wall of reserve beginning to build and backed off. Watching the crate of kittens leave her house was about as far as the woman would go today.

"Mommy's sorry," she said to them as Eric carried them out the door. "They know what that means," she said to no one in particular.

Des turned the conversation to the next step, to something pragmatic and logical, away from the emotional.

"What we need to do now," he said to the woman, who

fretted that the mother cat did not have a blanket, "is to figure out a plan." The remaining cats in the household would need to be vaccinated, he explained. The pregnant cats, who had sought the privacy of the mysterious basement, with its many nesting places, needed to be segregated. And finally, he needed a list of what supplies she most urgently needed to keep things under control in the interim.

"Everything," she said simply.

Food? She nodded yes. Kitty litter? Yes again.

"These people are delaying their own needs because of the cats," says Des, noting the total absence of food on the kitchen counters. He understands the impetus to take care of a cat in need, even if it means risking his own comfort or safety. One night in August of 2007, Des was awakened in the middle of the night by a call from someone who heard mewing in the elevator shaft of his Harlem apartment building.

Arriving equipped, Des pried open the elevator doors with a crowbar and shone his flashlight three stories down on a dirt-covered gray-and-white male cat. Tying a length of nylon rope to a heating pipe in the hallway, Des scaled down the elevator bank from the first floor—hoping that no tenants summoned the elevator from where it was berthed five floors above him—and then had the caller lower a cat carrier down to him. It was a good night: The cat got his freedom, and Des escaped unscathed.

A few months later, in December, Des heard about a marmalade-colored cat who had created a nest for her kittens between the side of a building and a fence. The gap was only ten inches wide, far too narrow for anyone to crawl in. So Des bought a huge pair of bolt cutters, hopped the fence to the property next door, and cut a hole through the fence to get the kittens.

"I was vandalizing someone's private property and risking arrest," he muses. "But there are women rescuers who are even more hard-core. They risk everything—their well-being, their welfare, being evicted. You put yourself in some bad situations to help these animals."

There is without question a gender divide in animal rescue, and it is practically the Grand Canyon when it comes to cats. Perhaps one reason that many men gravitate toward dogs is because they are relatively uncomplicated and eager to please. Cats, with their fierce independence, are not so willing to give over their trust, or their cooperation.

Big Ant still rolls his eyes at the mention of his picture in *Cat Fancy* magazine, cuddling a cute kitten. Though he has two cats at home, he would have preferred to be immortalized while mugging with a pit bull.

"Guys are into dogs, and women are into cats—it's a cultural thing," Des reflects. "But before I ate sushi I used to think it was pretty yucky. I like it now because I actually tried it."

Before Rescue Ink embarked on the Moriches cat case, Des had tried to interest the guys in another one involving a low-income-housing complex on Long Island whose landlord had boarded up all the basement windows so the feral cats on the property couldn't have access to shelter. Rescue Ink routinely confronts dog owners who don't adequately care for their dogs, depriving them of food and shelter, he pointed out. Why can't the in-your-face approach also be applied to neighbors and building managers who are hostile to the presence of cat colonies?

"What you don't know about Des is that he's a ninja. He's going to go there at night and drink all their milk," joked Joe about the cat-hating landlord's apartment complex.

The riff got a laugh, but in the end Des's point still stood.

The solution to the feral cats that already exist is the one no one wants to hear: accepting the fact that feral cats will live among us, and taking responsibility for controlling their numbers by trapping, neutering, and returning them to their outdoor territories.

"Nobody wants cats on their property," Des explains, noting that the history of attempted feline extermination likely stretches back ten thousand years, which is about as long as cats have been domesticated. "The people who kill, relocate, and starve cats as the solution to the overpopulation have ten thousand years of history working against them. They do the same thing over and over again with the same negative results, as evidenced by the current number of feral cats living today. The well-meaning efforts of these people create a vacuum effect allowing other cats from nearby areas to move in to make use of the existing available resources. Attrition through sterilization (TNR), however, has been scientifically documented in a number of case studies to show overwhelmingly positive results, concluding that TNR is the only known humane and non-lethal solution proven to work effectively."

There's no magic bullet for the feral-cat problem—and the solution needs to come from within. Neighbors, landlords—everyone—must get behind the idea of coexisting with a colony. Caretakers, in turn, need to realize that scattering unsightly feeding pans and uneaten food over yards isn't very considerate to property owners. Instead, caretakers can create camouflaged feeding stations and place them strategically behind bushes and outbuildings.

Focusing on the big picture—almost a million feral cats locally whose future and well-being rest on small groups of overly dedicated but woefully underfunded advocates—can make even the most idealistic of rescuers faint.

And in the hoarding situation in Center Moriches, there was a very strong likelihood that once the woman relocated into a new place, she would again begin to accumulate cats and simply rekindle the problem. But Des is a pragmatist, and the household's cats needed help right away. He did not have the luxury of worrying about the what-ifs that lay ahead.

On the bright side, at least the woman recognized that she had a problem. "Sometimes with these cases you have an ongoing undercurrent of denial, which this woman doesn't seem to have," Des says. "Her willingness to relinquish animals is also an indication that she's a bit more realistic."

Despite that, the condition of the cats told a sad story. The woman admitted that there had been outbreaks of viral disease, and while she did not disclose any deaths, Des could not help but conclude that there had been. The young cat with the infected eye worried him—it could be a congenital problem, or an injury, or an infection such as chlamydia.

Then, of course, there was the sheer number of cats. Finding foster homes and spaces at no-kill shelters for more than 150 cats would be daunting at best—as was the idea of keeping the cats separate and identified when Rescue Ink returned to vaccinate them.

That was another problem for another day. For now the seven kittens were loaded into the van, headed toward the prospect of loving homes and being spayed or neutered so they wouldn't add to the overpopulation problem. A small victory, but in a battle this protracted and fierce, rescuers take any victory they can get.

The ride home was relatively quiet. Someone asked again about the deep gash on Des's brow, and this time he answered.

"It's from a cat," he explained. Des had bent over to greet a male cat he had placed in foster care who did not know him well, and the cat struck out to defend himself against a perceived attack. For once, there was no ribbing, no wisecracks. It was a wound gained honorably, in the pursuit of loving an animal. Almost in unison, several guys in the van cautioned Des to have a doctor look at it before it became infected.

But from Des's point of view, it's just a symptom of a far more serious condition he's contracted. "Cat rescue is like a virus," says Des placidly about the cat obsession that has taken over his life. "And once you're infected, it's incurable."

5

Spike

New Year, New Beginnings

Spike was off to a good start. Or so it seemed.

At five months old, the bundle of brindled fur went to the vet. He got all his shots and a shiny silver rabies tag in the shape of a bone. As important as having his vaccinations, this Rottweiler–pit bull mix had the hopeful love of a nine-year-old boy who held and cuddled him in a house that, though it was run-down and had seen better days, was warm and safe. The boy dreamed about the dog Spike would grow up to be—a loyal companion who would never leave his side, a constant source of affection in a hardscrabble neighborhood where many boys had stopped dreaming long ago.

Two years later, on a bitter December night between the 2008 Christmas and New Year's holidays, the Rescue Ink van pulled up to Spike's house in Roosevelt, Long Island. The van carried everyone but Eric, who had to work. At the far edge of the backyard, beyond the crumbling concrete steps to the house, past a broken trampoline and a souped-up Mercedes, was a five-foot-square chain-link pen. A flimsy blue tarp covered it, flapping with every gust of icy wind.

And inside, pacing and growling in the muck of his own excrement, was Spike.

Dusk was falling, but the seven men could see clearly from the street that this was a case most rescue groups would run, not walk, from. Spike had been confined in the small pen for so long that he spun in circles obsessively, flinging himself against the chain link with every revolution. He had no doghouse; his only option was to curl up in the mud in which he paced all day.

G walked up to the pen, and Spike growled ominously, hackles raised, eyes hard and menacing. G didn't flinch as the enraged dog threw himself against the chain link, teeth flashing. Spike was sending a message. But so was G: He wasn't about to back down either.

Joe rang the bell, and the boy, now eleven years old, and his mother came outside. They were more than happy to part with Spike, the mother explained. The family was moving to North Carolina in a few days, and the snarling, feces-encrusted dog in the pen was not joining them in their new start.

"There was all this hustle and bustle, and he got caught in the middle," explained the boy's mother about how other priorities had overshadowed caring for Spike. She handed Big Ant the records of Spike's first—and only—visit to the vet. The silver tag was still tucked in the envelope, shiny and new.

That promising little puppy had transformed slowly but steadily into the aggressive monster in the cage that almost everyone was afraid to touch. As he grew bigger and got underfoot in the small apartment, he spent some time outdoors in the pen. Slowly, his time there increased, and he lost what few manners he had learned. His coat became crusted over with mud and feces, and he stayed outside full-time, even on the coldest and rainiest nights.

Over the summer, on one of his reprieves from the enclosure, he had bitten one of the boy's friends on the arm, and now he almost never left the pen, not even for a walk. The boy could open the gate to feed Spike and change his water, so the dog was in good weight. But the boy had long ago stopped cleaning out the feces in the pen. He just added more hay and latched the door.

"When you get a dog, you've got to socialize him," G said to the boy, who stared hard at a spot above G's shoulder as he talked. "You need to walk him around the block and have him meet new people, see new things. You have to spend fifteen minutes a day working with your dog. And I guarantee if you do, you'll have the most well-trained dog. He'll sit right by your leg and not move."

As Spike growled and snarled, the Rescue Ink members discussed logistics. They would be back at sunrise with a crate, and the boy and his stepfather would help load Spike inside it. Then Rescue Ink would drive off with Spike to his new life, whatever that was going to be.

As the discussion went on, the eleven-year-old stood a few feet away, staring stonily into the air. Hands jammed in his pocket, he stood ramrod straight. Batso walked over and touched the boy's shoulder. Just the sensation of the tattooed hand softened the facade that the boy had been trying so hard to maintain, and his eyes welled up.

Tears streaming down his face, he was likely thinking of Spike as a puppy, as the new arrival that had offered such promise and love. But that Spike was long gone, replaced by this vicious, teeth-flashing creature before them. And even the most optimistic of the Rescue Ink guys was hard-pressed to hope for too much of a storybook ending.

Aggressive dogs like Spike are the lost causes of the rescue world. With many shelters already overcrowded, no one has the time for or interest in rehabilitating a biter. It's a long, slow process, with no guarantee of success. And understandably, rescue groups are also concerned about the liability of placing a potentially aggressive dog in a home where a family member could unwittingly trigger a bite—or worse, perhaps a fatality.

Rescue Ink has rescued other dogs like Spike, and in tough cases like these, the guys turn to Eric Bellows of Train of Thought in Sprakers, in upstate New York. Over the last two years, Eric has worked with almost seven hundred "problem" dogs.

Eric believes in restoring a dog to balance using a "pack ethic." He believes that dogs are sensitive creatures who pick up on the imbalances of their human caretakers, and he directs all his efforts toward bringing the dogs to a calm state where they can act instead of react, and learn to behave appropriately.

But Eric is different from many pack-oriented trainers on a couple of key fronts. First, his rehabilitation facility is his own home. Eric, his wife, Keri Whitfield, his brother Jay, and Keri's sister, Brooke, who is married to Jay, live on the twenty-five-acre property and work full-time on the care, rehabilitation, and placement of all their canine cases.

Perhaps most important, Eric does not rely on punishment to reach his canine charges. With his peach-colored goatee and steady, calm way, he has an infinite reservoir of patience for the broken-spirited and rage-racked dogs who cross his threshold. He will not push, or overwhelm, or "flood" dogs with what they fear to get them to do what he wants. He just waits until they are ready to learn, and then, with the help of his resident pack of twenty dogs, shows them how to regain their calm, their control, and in the process, their dignity.

"Animals are not born fearful, nervous, anxious, or aggressive. Instead, the environment in which they are born influences their makeup entirely," Eric explains. "From the minute that he comes into this world, a dog's personality is in the ongoing process of development, moment to moment, every day."

From the sound of things, sheer neglect could have made Spike human-aggressive, Eric thought. In other words, the reason Spike was in the pen was not that he was aggressive; instead, being in the pen was what made him aggressive.

"Dogs who have been mistreated by humans, or even lack of exposure to humans, can develop fear-based aggressive tendencies," Eric says. "These dogs lack a basic trust for the actions and intentions of humans."

The first step, then, is to regain that lost trust. For a dog as shell-shocked as Spike, that means showing him that humans pose no threat. Then Eric begins to kindle a desire in the dog to see Eric as a leader, reconnecting him to his ancestral role as a follower in the domesticated pack, with the human in charge.

But all this is getting too far ahead of things. For right now, Spike needed to get from his pen to a crate, and then go to the vet to be neutered. Because sex hormones make dogs more competitive and edgy, Eric requires that any dog that trains with him and his pack at Train of Thought be altered first.

The Rescue Ink guys piled into the van and pulled away,

wondering who would lose an appendage in tomorrow morning's Operation Free Spike.

At seven the next morning, as the treeline behind Spike's pen became suffused with light, Big Ant and Joe pulled up to the tired white house. The stepfather looked in disbelief at the wire crate that Spike would be transported in. It was in fact the appropriate size—just large enough for the dog to stand, turn around, and lie down in—but the man seemed incredulous that the dog would enter it.

No one Spike didn't know could be in his view while the transfer took place, he warned. Spike would become too enraged. So Big Ant and Joe hopped back into the van and watched through the windshield as the boy and stepfather unlatched the gate.

Ecstatic to be free, Spike walked right into the crate. It was too easy.

Big Ant and Joe left the van and walked over to the crate near the pen. At the sight of them, the dog exploded into a fusillade of growls. Distracting him first on one end of the crate, then the other, they threaded some heavy rope through the gaps between the metal bars.

Big Ant put one hand near the crate and counted to five. He extended the other hand. "Six-seven-eight-nine-ten," he said to no one in particular. "They're my fingers—I want to keep them."

With a heave, Big Ant and Joe lifted the crate by the rope into the back of the van.

"Good-bye, big guy," the stepfather said to the wide-eyed dog. The boy stood by and watched as the door closed.

Big Ant and Joe were relieved that Spike was finally free from his miserable existence inside the pen. But it bothered them that the boy was learning the wrong lesson: After all the family's irresponsibility in caring for the dog, Rescue Ink had swooped in and cleaned up their mess. And they worried that the family would simply get another dog, and repeat the mistakes they had made with this one.

"You know, if you get another dog, you can't keep him in that pen," Big Ant said. "It's no way for a dog to live."

The stepfather bristled. "I don't like how that sounds," he said. "And I'm reading the side of your van, it says animal abuse. I didn't abuse no dog."

Joe and Big Ant didn't argue the point; it didn't look as if Spike's owners wanted any education. Rescue Ink had Spike, and that was all that mattered. And they would come around again to see if the family really did leave, or if the North Carolina relocation was a made-up story to get Rescue Ink to hurry up and take the dog.

Inside the van, Spike was already making his presence known; the choking scent of dog crap permeated the air.

Settling into the passenger seat, Joe took a whiff. "Eau de Midnight Pasture," he deadpanned.

"The owner was broken up and pissed off at the same time," Big Ant said, glancing at the side-view mirror as he pulled away from the house. "But locking a dog up like that so all he can do is watch the world go by—that's a form of abuse, too."

"Now it's not their problem, it's our problem," Joe concluded. "And we're going to handle it better than they did."

Spike had a few hours to settle in before his neutering appointment.

The vet tech who answered the phone at Island Park Animal Hospital had warned that if Spike could not be handled, he would need to come in with a muzzle. Joe pondered this for a while; even if they could find a basket- or box-style muzzle that fit correctly—a nylon muzzle would fit too tightly, impede his breathing, and make the dog stress out even more—he had no idea how he would put it on the dog.

Joe went out to the van and opened the rear door. Spike looked at him and growled, low and long, like he meant it.

Joe isn't an animal behaviorist, so he did the only thing he knew how to do in this case: He put himself in the dog's place and imagined how he would feel, something most experts would dismiss as anthropomorphizing. Joe thought about Spike's experience in human terms—what it would feel like to have been unjustly imprisoned for a decade in a small cell, forced to lie in his own urine and excrement, with little contact with the outside world, vulnerable to the teasing of kids.

Joe knew exactly how he'd feel. "This dog is pissed off," he concluded simply. "You know what they say: It's better to be pissed off than pissed on. Well, this dog was both."

Spike watched him warily from the cage. Every time Joe moved his hand, the dog tracked it with his eyes. Joe drew his hand closer to the side of the wire crate, and Spike lunged, putting his mouth up to the thin metal bars and issuing a growl from deep within his chest. "This dog's gonna be all right," said Joe, imagining himself again in the dog's place. In his current state, Spike was at least warm for the first time in a long time, and in a clean crate away from his own filth. That had to be an improvement.

But optimism aside, Joe couldn't imagine how he'd manage to put a muzzle on Spike at this point. If he let the dog out of the crate, he wasn't sure if he'd tolerate being on a leash, or if he'd go back in. Better to leave the genie in the bottle, at least for now.

Joe put his hand up to the crate again. This time, Spike did not snap. Slowly, steadily, Joe moved his fingers around the crate, near the side of Spike's head, and touched him. Spike sat silently as Joe's fingers petted him through the bars, scratching behind his ear. It was a small success, but Joe would take it.

A few hours later, Big Ant and Joe found themselves peering into the closet-size operating room at Island Park Animal Hospital.

Subduing Spike had turned out to be a cinch. The vet, Dr. Ratner, just injected him in the rump with a presurgical sedative through the crate as someone distracted him. Within fifteen minutes, Spike was punch-drunk and in no shape to inflict any harm. Coaxed out of the crate and then covered with an old comforter so he couldn't bite, Spike had lain down contentedly as Dr. Ratner found a vein for the induction anesthesia. Wrapped up in the comforter, Spike snored loudly.

Now here he was on his back on the operating table. Small droplets of blood had formed around the incision site; he had been so caked with dirt and grime that his skin was irritated from the vet tech's efforts to scrub and disinfect the area.

"This is the part that makes men cringe because it's so easy," said Dr. Ratner cheerily.

As Joe and Big Ant looked on, she made a small cut just above the testicles, then pushed one of them out of the scrotum and through the incision. Cutting the membrane that encased it, she yanked on the testicle, which was covered by a tough white ligament called the gubernaculum.

Big Ant was horrified. "How hard are you going to pull?" he asked.

"It looks like a dumpling," Joe interjected. "Now I'm getting hungry."

"You don't just put them in the garbage, do you?" Big Ant asked in genuine disbelief, as Dr. Ratner finished removing the gubernaculum, snipped off the testicle, and began to stitch.

"Do you want them?" asked Dr. Ratner, offering to preserve the relics of Spike's manhood in formaldehyde.

Big Ant demurred.

The second testicle was removed just like the first, except for Joe's musings that it looked like an egg. (If Joe doesn't eat every three hours or so, he either crashes or gets cranky, and lunchtime was long past due.)

"Just drop it in slow, with a little bit of dignity," Ant protested as Dr. Ratner plunked the second testicle into the wastebasket with a thud of finality.

As Dr. Ratner finished stitching Spike, a vet tech popped in and asked if she and her assistant wanted in on the lunch order. "They don't want a meatball hero, that's for sure," Ant muttered.

When Big Ant and Joe came back to pick Spike up after a couple of hours, the dog was snoozing in his crate, which was now lined with a clean towel. His nails were newly clipped, and he had received all his shots as well as a heartworm test.

This time he didn't growl as they lifted the crate into Joe's SUV; the Rescue Ink van, with its mismatched tires and temperamental brakes, wouldn't survive a trip to the frozen north,

where a snowstorm and twelve inches of snowfall were pre-
dicted for the next day, New Year's Eve.

"The sun's trying to poke through," commented Big Ant as
he headed north for the four-hour drive to Eric Bellow's place.

"Poke." Joe laughed appreciatively. No Rescue Ink exchange
can go on for long without the inevitable locker-room guffaw.

For most people who hear trainers talking about a dog's
"energy," it sounds sort of like a woo-woo word, something you
might hear from a fortune-teller or on a late-night infomercial.

But for Eric Bellows, energy is real and visceral, as powerful
as an electrical current. He can feel it wash over him when he
enters the garage kennel where his new arrivals live until they
are ready to transition into the house proper. And he is careful
to monitor and adjust his own energy so that it does not ignite
any "pack attack" among his more unstable charges.

Training aggressive dogs "really makes you think about
who you truly are, and how much ability you have to control
your emotions," he says. "If I get up in the morning and feel
tired, I take an extra ten to twenty minutes to revitalize myself
and shake it off before I walk into my pack. You can take five
deep breaths and change your entire frame of mind."

Given that dogs are so in tune with the energy around
them—and unbalanced, reactive dogs even more so—Eric considers attempting to evaluate them in the high-pressure, tense
shelter environment to be simply, patently unfair.

Spike's display of aggression in his pen at his old home was
also not a true reflection of who Spike is and what his temperament is like, Eric suggests.

"No matter if it's good or bad, the environment a dog

grows up in is consistent. That's what they get used to, and what they live for," he explains. "When you take them from that, or introduce new people or smells, they are automatically ripped out of what they feel safe in, and they're going to go into protection mode because they feel vulnerable."

Once the dogs are placed in a safe, low-stress environment like his facility, "we get to see who these dogs really are," Eric explains. "Too many people don't get to see that. And they're costing good dogs their lives."

Monster is a three-year-old Rottweiler whom Eric saved from a kill shelter in the Bronx. At nine months old, the black dog with the rust-colored markings had a nasty case of food and toy aggression, and was scheduled to be euthanized.

The first time they met, their eyes locked, and "he threw himself at me exuberantly," Eric remembers. "I never had a dog want me to lead him so badly before."

Days after his adoption, Monster accompanied Eric to the doggie day-care and training center where he worked. But when a staffer tossed a raw knuckle bone into the garbage, Monster dove after it, so possessive that he cleared the reception area of people and dogs. Eric entered the room, and Monster issued a low growl. Eric walked straight toward him, wrapped his arm around the dog's head, almost in a headlock, and just held him there, waiting for Monster to relinquish the bone. After fifteen minutes of "Give it, drop it, leave it" from Eric, and a few more growls from Monster, the dog dropped the bone into Eric's hand. Eric put the bone down, looked at the dog, and waited. Deferentially, Monster turned his head away, and a pact of trust was sealed.

Today, Monster is Eric's ever-present sidekick. "By reading his reactions, I know what to expect from dogs and people," he says. "And there are some situations with dogs that I wouldn't have been able to handle without Monster. He has a presence about him, and he can break the ice."

Eric's hope was that as Spike watched his interactions with Monster—or any of the twenty-some new arrivals in his facility—he would come to the conclusion that he too wanted that kind of trust and commitment from a human.

The first step, a baby step, would be to see if Spike was willing to follow him on a leash. "Fearful dogs resist this type of manipulation," he says. "Even getting a slip lead over their head and moving them can become the most difficult task."

Eventually, Eric would lead Spike into a whole new world. He would test him to see if he had hidden aggressions that a hapless owner might trigger, like Monster and that throwaway bone. He would teach him basic commands, get him to accept being bathed and groomed. And then Spike would move to Eric's house itself, where all the testing and training would be put to practical use, in preparation for finding a new home where he would finally, unconditionally, be loved.

At midnight, Joe's truck lurched along Eric's seemingly endless driveway. Though dense darkness surrounded them, they still got a sense of the wide-open feel of the property. Compared to the twenty-five square feet where Spike had lived for more than a year, this felt like heavenly infinity.

When they opened the back door of the truck, Spike looked at them expectantly. He was still a little groggy from the anesthesia, but not enough to prevent him from biting if he felt like it.

Eric walked over to the crate and held a small piece of string cheese between the bars.

Spike sniffed at it, then gingerly took it.

"Good boyyyyy," said Eric softly, drawing out the "oi" sound. "He's using his nose—that's a very good sign," he added. It meant that Spike was taking the time to investigate and explore his surroundings and not just react. Eating is not compatible with outbursts of emotion; no one with an adrenaline rush feels like chowing down.

Eric offered another piece of cheese, and Spike took it a little more eagerly this time.

Now came the big test: removing Spike from the crate.

The three men decided that straightforward was best. Joe opened the crate door and waited.

Spike did nothing.

Joe took a looped lead and slowly slipped it over Spike's head.

Still, the dog lay motionless in the crate.

Joe handed the leash to Eric, who gave it a gentle tug. Spike stood and contemplated the distance from the tailgate to the ground.

With Eric murmuring words of encouragement, Spike moved to the very edge of the crate and then jumped, landing effortlessly on his feet.

Big Ant and Joe watched with equal measures of satisfaction and incredulity as Eric walked Spike toward some nearby pine trees to relieve himself. He gave the dog lots of slack leash, and Spike wandered contentedly, like a tourist.

"He's a wicked good boy," said Eric of the dog who just that morning looked like he would chew up and spit out anyone who dared approach him. Just from this brief encounter,

Eric got the strong sense that Spike would be quickly transformed into a calm, obedient house pet, perhaps in as little as a month. "There is a wonderful dog underneath all the pent-up stuff."

Eric walked Spike back to the men at the rear of the truck. Spike looked up at Big Ant and Joe and managed a hesitant tail wag.

It lasted only a moment, but to them it was an eternity.

6

Batso

Age Is Just a Number

The Rescue Ink guys sat in the Catholic chapel, waiting for the seats to fill.

Behind them, at the back of the room, life-size statues of the Virgin Mary and Saint Joseph looked on, their marble visages impenetrable. Over the last sixty years, they had witnessed generation after generation of street toughs. By comparison, these visiting animal rescuers were pretty much choirboys.

Rescue Ink had been invited to Saint John's Residence for Boys in Rockaway Park, a residential school for teenage boys, to talk to the students about animal rescue and abuse, and being a responsible owner. Every Rescue Ink member had turned out for this speaking engagement in a hardscrabble Queens neighborhood on the shore of the Atlantic Ocean. Des, Eric, G, Angel, and Johnny O sat on the left side of the chapel, in front of the altar. Big Ant and Batso shared a Gothic antique oak pew on the right. Joe was standing, because if he wasn't, he would be tapping his foot furiously, unable to contain his energy.

Sitting against one of the chapel walls, Mary, next to Bruce, held Luigi the geriatric Maltese in her arms. She'd dressed him in pale blue pajamas, but the guys had demanded she remove them. To these street-savvy teenagers, hardened by life and just a step away from a jail sentence, appearances are everything. Toothless and trembling, Luigi didn't need to amplify his wimpy image any further.

With its narrow, high-ceilinged hallways and closet-size classrooms, the interior of the hulking brick building felt a bit like the inside of a submarine. Before it was a reform school, it had been an orphanage. To brighten things up in the windowless hallways, inspirational pictures and posters hung on the walls and doors. "Just when the caterpillar thought the world was ending," read one, "he turned into a butterfly."

Batso, who at seventy-five is the group's oldest member, looked around, impressed. He had been sent to a reform school as a thirteen-year-old because of his constant fighting and disruptiveness at school. But back then, in the 1940s, they called it a "workshop." Instead of studying under the watchful eyes of a teacher, he had been sentenced to a year of hard labor picking tobacco in his home state of Connecticut. At night, the boys slept on hard boards, not mattresses, and fistfights punctuated the hours of the night.

So compared to what Batso knew, this was heaven. And he'd be sure to tell the boys so when he got the chance.

Batso stops traffic. It really is as simple as that.

Of all the Rescue Ink guys, Batso, whose birth name is Nicholas Maccharoli Sr., is the most heavily tattooed. His head and face draw the most attention. From the benevolent

Buddha on his bald pate to the tiny spiderweb in his ear, from the barbed wire circling his neck to the colony of his namesake bats that take flight on his skull, there's little of Batso's head that remains uninked.

Though he is a first-generation Italian-American whose parents immigrated before World War II, Batso has an Eastern air, from his Fu Manchu pigtail to his fierce brown eyes, which evoke a Mongolian warrior. He drinks high mountain oolong tea procured from small dusty shops in Manhattan's Chinatown, and takes the Chinese herb astragalus, used for millennia to strengthen and energize the body. And like the Chinese tradition he has embraced—which holds that everything contains the yin and the yang, the dark and the light, the contemplative and the reactive—Batso too has a deep, abiding duality.

But in the first three-quarters of his life, he says, he knew nothing about the importance of balance and harmony in one's body and spirit. One of his first childhood memories is being tied to a tree by his mother, who, frustrated with the second youngest of her six children, could not control him. She used to hit him regularly with a broom handle, like a dog. "Bang, bang, bang," he remembers of those blows. "I was bad. I never knew how to read or write. I used to fight all the time—I didn't know any better."

Batso's relationship with education was not a long-lived one: He smoked cigarettes in the school bathroom and threatened bodily harm to the teachers, including a nun whose propensity for corporal punishment matched that of his mother. After fifth grade, he never went back.

Right after reform school, Batso found a trade. He became a body man, doing finishing work on cars. He spent five years sanding and stripping cars with paint remover and a putty knife. "Then one of the old-timers showed me how to hold a hammer," Batso says. "He picked me up in the air and said, 'You little hoodlum, I'm gonna make a body man out of you.'" True to his word, he showed Batso how to hold a hammer and strike the metal, then pick and file it to remove the dent—a lost art today, when most new cars would crumple under the force necessary to reshape those vintage chassis. Batso's education was complete when he was shown how to apply the lead, melting it with a welding torch. "I learned everything by feel, I measured everything from feel," he remembers. "Even when I was mixing paint, I could feel how much thinner to put in to reduce the paint." Consciously or not, it's a philosophy Batso has extended to working with animals; sensing their energy, he is able to connect with them on a level far beyond pats on the head or scratches under the chin.

Today, Batso's house in suburban Connecticut is filled with the artwork he has painted—smiling, contented Buddhas in all stages of their life journey, from sheltered prince to meditative master. But back in his younger days, he expressed himself not with a paintbrush but with his cars. Parked in Batso's garage are three automobiles he customized himself: a red-and-white 1957 Ford convertible with an airbrushed angel scene and the words *Calling All Angels* scripted across the back. An eggplant purple 1950 Ford with a King Tutankhamen theme and its very own mummy coffin. And, his masterpiece, the Bat's Revenge, a labor of love that took four years: The black 1951 Ford has bat-shaped parking lights, wheel spinners, and back window, and a front grille cut to resemble teeth. Batso was once offered $150,000 for the car, but turned it down. After all, it wasn't just a car. On some level, it was an extension of himself.

In Batso's basement is a framed photo of him as an eighteen-year-old. He is pictured inside a 1939 Ford with a raccoon tail tied to the antenna. Batso himself looks unremarkable, like any young man in the early 1950s in slacks and a shirt, hair combed back in a DA haircut. A half century later, just as he's done with his vintage cars, Batso has transformed himself from that fresh-scrubbed young man to a walking piece of art. His unorthodox appearance has earned him a recurring role as part of the biker gang on the HBO prison series *Oz*, and he had a bit part in the celebrated Mickey Rourke movie *The Wrestler*.

"When you do crazy stuff, you're more noticeable. You expose yourself. You stand out in a crowd," Batso says about his decision to cover himself in tattoos. "I wanted to be something. You know why? Because I came out of nothing. I wanted to be something before they put the dirt on me."

But his outrageous appearance is a double-edged sword. Whenever he is in public, invariably someone will point to his tattooed face and ask, "Did it hurt?" or "Why did you do that?" Even benign questions like that, and the stares and the pointing, annoy him. "I get condemned a lot for the way I look," he complains. People judge, without knowing even one thing about him.

Slowly, the Saint John's students shuffled into the room. They were all youth and attitude, pants slung low, backpacks flung over their shoulders. Clumped in groups of twos and threes, the boys filled the back seats first, avoiding those in front where the teachers could see them best.

Rescue Ink had done many school presentations before

coming to Saint John's, but never to a crowd this tough. When speaking to suburban grade-schoolers, the Rescue Ink guys explain how important it is to protect every animal by reporting abuse to a parent, teacher, or policeman. They ask the kids to be their eyes and ears when they aren't around. The emphasis is placed on being helpful and doing the right thing, and at the end, Angel swears them all in as Official Junior Pet Investigators. But that approach clearly wasn't going to fly here, where just the weekend before four of the boys had been arrested for robbing a neighboring home.

"We're trying to touch the kids and let them know that they're not forgotten and that we're here to give them a second chance, just like some of the dogs we rescue," G explained to a visitor as the room filled even more, and the front seats began to get occupied.

Several of the young men looked at Luigi and pointed, smiling. Without missing a beat, Mary handed him over to a plump young student who looked as if he had just been given a pint-size alien. Gingerly, he held Luigi in his hands, mindful of his small size and delicate frame. And though some of his tougher schoolmates murmured some cracks under their breath, they too kept stealing glances at goofy-looking little Luigi, whose mere presence seemed to settle and focus these agitated young men.

"He has no teeth," Mary said cheerfully when a boy asked why the dog's tongue lolled out of his mouth to the left. "That's why his tongue keeps falling out."

A school administrator strode to the front of the room, and with a raised voice, shushed the boys. One by one, the Rescue Ink members stood up and introduced themselves, and talked for a few minutes. Joe introduced the group as a bunch of street guys who take an "in-your-face approach" to animal abuse and neglect. Johnny O talked, as he always does, about pit bulls and how they are overbred and underappreciated.

G's message was about change, and how it is always a possibility at any time, for anyone. "You guys are in the situation that you're in because you didn't think about what you were doing," he explained. "I'm forty years old now, but when I was your age, I did some things that I may have regretted." But the point, he concluded, was that first he chose to change, and then he did. It is never too late.

Eventually, it was Batso's turn. He stood up, and a quiet rumble went through the room as the young men took in his tattooed face and head.

"My name is Batso," he started off, jutting out his chin as if expecting to hear an objection. "I came from a reform school back in my day. They didn't call it that, though, they called it a workshop. I picked tobacco. It was one year's hard labor on a farm. We had no beds. We slept on benches, with little blankets over them. And I had no life. I couldn't read or write. I was a bully, worse than you guys. I was fighting and doing everything."

The room was still, as the students surveyed Batso and imagined him in his prime. "But now, I'm here to help animals, and I'm here to help you guys," he continued. "You know, you don't want to turn out to be like me. It's like no life. It's like being in the dark. You know, you guys got a good head on your shoulders. Once you get involved with animals, it's gonna calm you down and make you relax, and make you forget about a lot of things."

Batso drew out that last phrase softly, and spread out his hands, as if smoothing a rumpled blanket.

Science backs up what Batso believes about the healing power of animals. Studies of Alzheimer's patients and children with behavior disorders and Down syndrome all show that the presence of animals has a calming effect, helping dispel anger and aggression and promote focus and positive interaction.

"Me, I had no life," Batso continued. "Now I learned. In my sixties and seventies I have a better life, I got involved with my boys over here"—he pointed to the other Rescue Ink guys—"and they took good care of me.

"I'm seventy-five years old," concluded Batso. At this, there was a burst of conversation and feet thumping, as the young men became incredulous that he was old enough to be their grandfather. "And I know how to handle myself," said Batso, wanting them to know that even though he was an old man by anyone's definition, he was tough enough to stand up to anyone, even a bunch of young punks. "You know what I mean?"

Then Batso sat down and looked out at the boys, wondering if they did.

Even as a boy, Batso was always an animal lover. He wanted a dog, but his mother forbade it, saying he couldn't have one where they lived, in the slums of Bridgeport, Connecticut. So instead he found a stray dog and tied her to a streetlight outside. The dog barked all night long, waking up the neighborhood, for which Batso's father beat him.

Like Big Ant, Joe, and Johnny O, today Batso owns a pit bull. She's a low-slung blond beauty named Inka who likely has a drop of Labrador retriever in her family tree. Her ears are indecisive, sometimes pointing straight up, sometimes folded over, and sometimes crinkled. In April 2008, Rescue Ink had been called to rescue the emaciated Inka after she had been tied to a bench in the rain in Brooklyn for four days. Batso, allergic to dogs, wasn't sure he wanted her, but the guys pressed him. G, who also lives in Connecticut and usually accompanies Batso to the Rescue Ink events by train, volunteered to help take Inka home with them on the ferry. Batso's wife Elly has a photo of that historic ride in a scrapbook she made for the now plump pit.

Today Inka spends most of her time on a wide window ledge at the front of the house, contentedly watching the traffic pass or snoozing in a shaft of sunlight. She is Batso's constant companion, following him around looking for treats, for which she is willing to work. "Roll over for Daddy," Batso will say. And Inka will fling her chubby seal-like body onto the floor, and gyrate accordingly.

"I have an idea for a T-shirt," says Batso, who has already begun to draw the design. It's a pit bull holding a tattoo needle, which has begun to script out the words: "Rescue Ink. Rescue Me."

Inka is not only Batso's muse for projects such as these, but somewhat of a child to him as well. On Halloween he dressed her as a pirate and brought her to Manhattan for the annual Greenwich Village parade. She solicited as many pictures as he did, which was nice for a change. The pirate dress and dog sunglasses with skull and crossbones are just one of her costume changes. She also has a yellow slicker for rainy days and a crocheted pink sweater with ruffle trim when more formal attire is called for.

"I walk with her up to the church every night, and sometimes when no one's there I take her in," Batso says. In the stillness among the pews, he has taught her how to say her prayers by tucking her nose under her front paws. It's a trick, but there's also a deeper thought there: Batso sees a spark of the divine in all animals, which is what draws him to them so strongly.

Sometimes, Batso takes Inka to the grave of his son Nicholas Jr., who died in January 2007 of Lou Gehrig's disease at the age of forty-seven. Batso raised Nicholas Jr., as well as his younger son Michael and stepson Johnny, the hard way, just as he had been raised, with a strong hand. He didn't know any better. "I put a roof over their heads, and food on the table," Batso says, the regret and grief creeping into his voice, "but not much else." The two discussed Batso's absence as a father when Nicholas Jr. was on his deathbed, "and Nick said, 'Don't worry about it, I'm with you all the time.'"

Still, thinking about it, sometimes Batso gets a piercing feeling in his gut, "like someone stabbed me." And when that happens, he settles down in his red-painted living room, facing the Chinese cabinet with two Fu lions—a shrine to his son, who, like his father, was a martial artist—that dominates the wall. While Inka keeps him company, taking up her post on the windowsill, "I put music on and light candles," Batso says. "It is so beautiful, so relaxing, to just let your whole body go, like dropping a tissue and watching it float down through the air."

Batso's first wife died of leukemia thirty-five years ago. Batso met his second wife, Elly, when he was forty-seven and she was nineteen. "I had a long beard, long stringy hair, I looked like an old man on a mountain, I looked ready to die," he remembers. She was a teller at the bank where he paid his mortgage.

He got her phone number by telling her he was thirty-seven. She in turn added one year to her real age, and in this way, by mutual white lies, they narrowed the chronological gulf between them. Their ages were immaterial; what mattered was the connection between them.

When Batso turned fifty-nine, Elly bought him a membership to a gym, "and it was like being born over again," he says. He soon got into martial arts and weightlifting. At age sixty, he took second place in the Master Light division at the Connecticut Open Power Lifting Championships, creating a state record that still holds today. He can pull one hundred pounds with his neck. And on any given day, he might run two hours on the treadmill, or do as many minutes on the rowing machine.

It wasn't until the sixth or seventh decade of his life, Batso says, that the yin part of life—the quiet, the contemplative, the nurturing—began to make itself known to him.

Wanting to get closer to the earth, Batso began to make his own soap out of all-natural ingredients: olive oil, oatmeal, coconut oil, shea butter, ginseng, honey, green tea, and vitamin E. "It's good stuff. Especially if you get hungry," jokes Big Ant. The soap-making started as a necessity, as Batso was allergic to most commercial soaps. But now he hopes to make a business of it, pressing his handmade soaps into bat molds and selling them under the name "BatsoAP."

When he started working out, he also began to eat well. He still avoids sugar, eats organic produce, and drinks lots of Chinese tea. Women often exclaim over his smooth skin; he looks decades younger than he is. But Batso's transformation is also spiritual: Once he began to strengthen and purify his body, he started to explore energy medicine, trying to feel the invisible meridians where the Chinese tradition says the animating life force moves across the body.

Batso had always been curious to see if animals would respond to some of the Chinese practices he uses on himself. In January 2009, Johnny O visited a Long Island family with a partially paralyzed miniature longhaired dachshund. The owner, who was a friend of Johnny's, was at the end of his rope with six-year-old Brownie. The dog had had surgery for debilitating back pain and the loss of control of his rear legs. Now the pain had receded, but his back legs still frequently collapsed beneath him. Brownie had no bowel control, and the family had long ago removed most of the area rugs because he had ruined them. The surgeon had recommended hydrotherapy, but the family balked at the expense. And now they were wondering if they should find a new home for little Brownie, who could not navigate the many stairs in their split-level home.

Batso got the chance to try some healing therapies on the animal when he accompanied Johnny on the visit. He held Brownie on his lap and gently stroked the dog's back. Gently, he tried to find the pressure points on Brownie's legs that might help his energy circulation. In his study of Chinese culture and medicine, Batso had learned about the concept of chi, the life energy that animates us all. It travels in channels, or meridians, throughout the body, and energy can either be released or drawn in, and balance restored, by stimulating certain points along the meridians.

"He was shaking a little, and after a while the shaking stopped and I felt his energy relaxing to my energy," Batso says. "After a few minutes he was so relaxed and he felt good. Real good."

Animals have much to teach us about living in the moment, Batso adds. "I don't think Brownie has much pain today. He wasn't thinking about it, you know why? Because he took his mind off it because of us. If you're gonna think about pain, you're gonna have pain. Right? So this dog wasn't thinking about pain. He was happy all over when he saw us."

Batso gives advice to the Rescue Ink guys about what foods to eat and what supplements to try. Sometimes, he offers them a piece of the dried ginseng he carries in a little ziplock bag in his pocket, but they all make a face and wave him off, especially Big Ant. "They all think I'm going to poison them." Batso sighs.

But not all the guys think Batso's alternative ideas are nuts. When Joe was knocked off his motorcycle and sent flying into the asphalt by a minivan-driving mom who never stopped, he couldn't raise his left arm for days. A friend who is a Reiki master offered to send him some of the healing energy long-distance, while he slept. The next morning, Joe could finally raise his arm.

Joe didn't know what to think about his overnight transformation. The rest of the guys rolled their eyes, brushing it off as a lot of hocus-pocus. But Batso truly believed. He understands that energy medicine is a powerful form of healing, and that's what he thought Brownie needed. "You see, I believe in magic," he says. "I believe in miracles. That would be the best thing I've ever done in my life if I could make that poor dog walk a little better. Wouldn't that be great? And I'm thinking about it all the time."

Adding a little apple cider vinegar to Brownie's water might also help, he told the owners. Vinegar is a time-tested body tonic and might alleviate some of the arthritis he had in his spine and rear legs. "It helped me, I take it," he said. "You know, and maybe add some fish oil to his food. That's good lubrication for the bones."

He was livid at the idea that Brownie's family might put him down because of the difficulty of caring for him. If that turned out to be the case, he'd take Brownie himself, he declared. "I think this dog is going to make it. I don't want to hear about putting him down, I don't want to hear it. I don't go for that," Batso says.

Brownie's battle may seem like an uphill one, but Batso knows that sheer determination can take you places unimagined. In his seventh decade of life, he has committed himself to conquering his illiteracy. "I'm not giving up," he says. "I learned how to read, and I'm not ashamed of myself."

In small marble-print composition books, Batso painstakingly copies passages from books for young readers. "About 2,500 years ago there lived a man called Siddhartha Gautama," reads one entry, from a book about the Buddha. "Siddhartha was a royal prince." He has a private tutor and literacy volunteer who comes every week to help him along.

"Nick is an absolutely wonderful student," says Liz Franko, the literacy volunteer who has been tutoring Batso once a week at the public library for the last nine years. "I don't see the tattoos anymore, I just see the person"—a person whose dedication to learning and growing in his twilight years has impressed her deeply.

"A lot of people scribble," Batso muses. "But I print real good."

Sometimes he has difficulty with a word or grows impatient with himself for taking so long to read something. "I get so mad at myself," he says. Then again, he has come so far. And he has plans to keep on going as far and as long as his body will let him.

A week after he was first introduced to Brownie, Batso met the spunky little dachshund again at the New York Veterinary Specialty Center in Farmingdale, where Rescue Ink had arranged for him to get some much-needed physical therapy. The paralyzed dog had been on his mind all week, he admitted.

Batso watched as Susan Marino, a canine physical therapist, carried Brownie into a hydrotherapy tank with her. Straddling the tank's treadmill, she pushed a button, and water filled the tank until it reached Brownie's chest. Then she pushed another button, and the treadmill beneath his feet began to move, at just over half a mile an hour.

Batso watched Brownie through the Plexiglas side of the tank. Made buoyant by the water, he was able to use his rear legs, however weakly. Brownie stayed in the tank for just under seven minutes, covering only a fraction of a mile.

When Brownie was done and the tank was drained, Susan wrapped him in a towel. "He's exhausted—he'll sleep well tonight," she said. The owners could continue the therapy in their own bathtub, since Brownie was small enough, she added.

Batso began talking about energy and chi, and Susan smiled in agreement. In addition to her therapy work, she runs a hospice for animals called Angel's Gate, which recently moved from Long Island to upstate Delhi, and holistic medicine is an underlying fundamental of her philosophy of care. A big believer in energy therapies, she showed Batso how to perform a healing therapy called the Tellington TTouch. By making small, deliberate circles with his fingertips on Brownie's skin, Batso could help open new neural pathways and teach the body to rewire itself neurologically.

But more than any therapy or holistic technique, Susan stressed, was what Batso believed. His conviction about helping Brownie was as powerful as any medicine. "To me, everything starts with intention," Susan explained. "If everyone sets the intention that this dog will walk again, he will."

"I believe it's going to happen," said Batso earnestly. "I know I'll make him walk. I can do it. I got time. It's all I got."

In many ways, Rescue Ink came into being powered largely by intention. Organizing eight men who are all strong-willed, hands-on, and never at a loss for opinions is sometimes akin to herding cats. The obstacles are constant; the donations don't come close to covering the costs of rescue operations, which inevitably come out of their own pockets. Their families are supportive but sometimes, understandably, become exasperated at the long hours and constant crises. Yet the group has managed to stay together simply out of sheer will.

Back at the reform school, after listening to the guys give their introductions, the students watched a film about Rescue Ink in which its members talk about what rescue means to them.

"My boys, these are like my children, 'cause I'm like the oldest," said Batso to the camera. "Rescue Ink means a lot to me. When it comes to animals, I love animals so much. Some of the stuff that we saw with how these people mistreat these animals, sometimes I have to walk away. I get so mad," he concluded, "I just want to *bite* them."

The idea of Batso taking a chomp out of an animal abuser

sent ripples of laughter through the room, because of the very real possibility that Batso just might.

Batso knows what some of these boys haven't quite figured out yet about new beginnings. Through sheer intention, desire, and determination he changed his life. "I only started to live in my sixties and seventies," says Batso. "It was like going back to being born. I brought myself back to being young again. My age is just a number."

The class period was over, and the young men began to file out. It was hard to tell if anything any of the guys said had gotten through to them.

"When people come to a place like this, the main thing the kids are going to hear is, 'You shouldn't do this or that.' They've heard it fifty times," Batso reflects.

Instead, he hoped they understood his heartfelt message: That it is never too late to alter the course of your life. That the animals can be a conduit to that transformation. And that out of respect comes love.

"Did we get through to you?" Batso asked the hard, youthful faces in front of him.

No one answered.

7

Joe Panz

The Wolves Within

Joe Panz waited in the Starbucks on Jericho Turnpike. Because he is the kind of guy who could break out in hives just from saying the word *frappuccino*, much less ordering one, he was drinking regular coffee with one Sweet'n Low, which always reminds him of that joke about the gay midget.

While the occasional arrival of Lycra-clad women for their postworkout lattes was a pleasant diversion on this crisp November day in 2008, Joe was keeping an appointment with one female stranger in particular.

From a car parked in the packed lot emerged a woman in her mid-fifties with permed blond hair and an air of hesitation. It had taken her two days to agree to this clandestine meeting. And no sooner had she shaken Joe's hand and introduced herself than she began to cry.

She had arranged to meet dozens of miles away from her home, across the county line, and still she felt vulnerable and afraid. Afraid that the wrong person would find out she had reached out for help.

"I want you to see some videos," said the woman, whom we'll call Sally, between sobs, handing Joe a bulging manila envelope.

Sally had explained to Joe on the phone that her backyard abutted that of an elderly man whose killing of animals had built steadily for a decade, and was now reaching alarming proportions. He baited his backyard with pounds of birdseed and peanuts, trapped the birds and animals, then killed them by drowning them or twisting their heads off. His yard was dotted with animal traps, and once his gruesome work was done, he lobbed dead birds and kittens into Sally's swimming pool or left dead possums in her shed.

Gleefully, he shot at squirrels scampering along the fence that divided their yards, she said, even at birds in midair.

"In the past, shots have come into my yard, putting holes in my fence and my house and breaking all my windows upstairs, including my bedroom, just a few feet away from where my head is in the bed," remembered Sally, who lives alone.

She called the police and the county SPCA, and while they issued summonses and arrested him on everything from harassment to animal cruelty, he never stayed incarcerated for long. She had an order of protection, as did her two neighbors. One of them had even moved away out of fear and frustration. And yet things just kept getting worse.

Rescue Ink learned about her situation from an e-mail Sally sent, and Joe gave Sally a call. "This guy is torturing us," said Sally. "Can you do something—anything?"

If Sally was looking for an advocate in an impossible situation, Joe Panz was as good as it gets. Part of that has to do with his imposing appearance. He gets up at four thirty every morning to go to the gym, where his routine would drop a Clydesdale: an hour and a half of cardio, hundreds of sit-ups, weightlifting, punching the heavy bag and speed bag, another half hour of cardio, and still more sit-ups for the road.

At thirty-nine, Joe Panz has two speeds: fast and faster. Constitutionally incapable of ignoring any opportunity for a double entendre, he is happiest when he is crossing the line, drop-kicking a gauntlet across the room. Like many of the Rescue Ink guys who page through hot-rod magazines featuring '50s-chignoned models in cashmere twin sets and belly rings, he is something of a throwback, with old-fashioned ideas about honor and what it means to be a man. When Joe goes to a diner, he orders wine and Diet Coke, then mixes the two. "It's an old Italian thing," he explains—the sweetness of the soda covers up the bitterness of wine that has passed its prime.

Joe Panz is, without question, the loudest member of Rescue Ink, but in his case, a raised voice does not bear any relationship to his level of anger. If he's truly enraged, he loses all words and becomes, like the stillness before a tornado, truly ominous.

Several months before his meeting with Sally, Joe went on a Rescue Ink call about a Long Island man who was keeping his three dogs in his car.

Joe's position in the Rescue Ink formation tends to be right next to the guy who is knocking on the door. There he stands, arms crossed, eyes fixed, like a bad dream.

The homeowner came to the door and explained that the dogs' owner was from Arizona and was staying with him until he got back on his feet.

"He has, you know, he has no money, he's got a job at Wal-Mart, and I'm trying to help him out, and I don't want the dogs in the house," he rambled, adding that the impending East Coast summer was brisk compared to the southwestern scorchers the dogs were accustomed to. The dogs had been in the car since November, the man explained. It was now May. "ASPCA has been here, is checking it all out, and everything's fine," he said in a garbled rush.

The Rescue Ink members who circled the Subaru Outback as the three dogs inside barked manically were obviously not concurring with the man's assessment of "fine." Joe decided to express his concerns, finger pointed, voice raised, with all the nuance of a cement truck.

"Would you want to be stuck in a car with the windows open this much? With five guys?" he demanded of the home-owner. "That's what I'm asking you—would you want that? To be stuck in a car with five guys with the windows open this much?"

"If that's gonna make you survive . . . ," the man ventured.

"I don't think you'd survive," retorted Joe, louder this time. "Why?"

Louder still, each word clipped like a hammer blow: "Because if I stuff you in a car with five guys with the windows open this much, I don't think you'd live for very long."

"Why?" asks the guy again, clueless.

And finally from Joe came the declaration that he uses so frequently the guys have threatened to have a shirt printed with it.

"Because I said so," he roared.

By this time, the police had arrived in response to the home-owner's call, as well as the local animal-welfare officer, and finally, the owner of the dogs. Tickets were written, the dogs were sprung from the vehicle, and Rescue Ink's "in-your-face" style resulted in "out-of-the-car dogs"—for that day, at least.

But, intimidation factor aside, there is another advantage to having Joe Panz as an ally, as Sally was soon to find out. He comes from a world where your word is everything, and he had promised Sally, as the cappuccino machine gurgled in the background, that he would help her.

There are neighborhoods, and then there are *neighborhoods*. Joe grew up in the kind where the once-modest ranches had been transformed into Corinthian-columned showplaces of brick arches and elaborate white ironwork. It was the kind of neighborhood where everyone painted the fire hydrants green, white, and red after Italy won the World Cup, where steely-eyed men sipped espresso in social clubs, and where the lowest form of humanity was a snitch.

Joe gives out information on a need-to-know basis. And what you need to know about him is that for as long as he can remember, he's been giving authority the finger. He was asked to leave first grade by the sisters at St. Helen's after an incident involving a fire extinguisher on which he'd rather not elaborate. By twelve, he was peddling illegal fireworks. He got thrown out of his Catholic all-boys high school sophomore year when he refused to rat out a friend. And by the time he was seventeen, his mother asked him to leave the house because she feared the company he kept would soon put one of his siblings in the crossfire.

Joe's body is an encyclopedia of war wounds. The lump on his hairline is courtesy of a bottle, the one over his eyebrow is from a baseball bat. The scar on his left thigh came from a knife, as did the one through his forearm and the one on his chest that he Krazy-Glued together.

But it is the six bullet holes—five entries, the sixth an exit wound from the one that pierced his chest—that made Joe who he is today.

It was a cold night more than a decade ago when an acquaintance pulled up alongside Joe's car and cajoled him into having a nightcap. Tired from an evening of partying, Joe initially said no, but his companion insisted until Joe eventually relented.

They went to an establishment where, had Joe not been so off his game, he would have noticed the strange stillness in the room. He stayed for a while, said good night, then headed to the door. That's when the shooting began.

"It's funny—I remember the hole of the gun, and the sparks," says Joe, who backed out of the bar and staggered to his car. There he waited for the second round.

Because the shooter had wrestled with Joe as he was shooting down at him, two bullets lodged in Joe's thighs and two in his lower back. Before the last one entered his chest, it hit the gold cross studded with rubies that had been his grandmother's. The bullet fragmented against the cross, which bent and embedded itself in Joe's chest, likely saving his life.

"When something like that happens, everything slows down," he says. "And you say to yourself, 'Moron, you better think as clear as possible, or you're going to die.'"

The door opened slightly, but no one came out. Instead, there was a pause, and the door closed against the night.

Joe knew the two places he absolutely could not go to were

his apartment and the hospital. Those would be the first places they would look for him to finish the job.

So he stopped at an acquaintance's house where he had a key, asked if he could crash, and got a sleepy yes. In the bathroom, he stuffed the hole in his chest with toilet paper, but every time he breathed, blood oozed out.

Somehow, he managed to sleep a few hours. But in his semiconsciousness, he heard the phone ringing and a whispered conversation about him. Within three hours of the shooting the sun had yet to rise, but word about his situation had already rippled through the neighborhood.

"Now I realize I have no one," Joe says simply. "Nobody going crazy in the street looking for who hurt me. Nobody rallying to help me. And I'm with this person I thought I could trust, but how do all these people on the phone know I'm here?"

Suffice it to say Joe Panz knows what it feels like to be alone.

Taking Sally's videotape out of the manila envelope, Joe settled down in his home office—a room with walls painted a color called Million Dollar Red, faux-zebra chairs, and an hourglass on the shelf—and popped in the tape.

Bond wandered in and settled himself on the floor at Joe's feet.

Several months before, during a Rescue Ink trip to the Town of Islip Animal Shelter on Long Island, Joe noticed a burly dog with a brindled gold coat that made him look like a tiger. The pit bull–bullmastiff mix had been dropped off months earlier, and with a head the size of a bowling ball and bulging muscles covering his body, he was simply too scary-looking to be an adoption prospect.

"I better take him before something bad happens to him," thought Joe, who told himself he was fostering the dog for a few days until a good home could be found.

A few days passed, then a few months, and eventually, the dog, whose shelter ID number ended in "007," became Bond, Joe Panz's dog.

"He's a big dog, and he's scary looking, but he has a good heart," concludes Joe.

On the TV the homemade tape rolled, showing an elderly man with a long white beard and hair tied in a ponytail—a bizarro Santa Claus—puttering around his yard with a large wire box. There was movement inside, a flash of white and gray—a rabbit. The bunny put its paws up on the trap's wire sides, looking for an exit.

The man set the trap on its side, opened it, reached in, and patiently grabbed at the wriggling rabbit until he secured it. Then he put his hands around the rabbit's neck until, several minutes later, it went limp. Methodically, eerily, he examined it, until it suddenly resuscitated, and then he began the slow, steady pressure again, seemingly enjoying the act of bringing the defenseless creature to the brink of death.

Then the tape cut to another scene—a different season this time, with the greening buds of spring instead of the ice-crusted shrubs of winter. This trap was filled with birds. One by one the old man removed them, held them on the pavement on the side of his house, severed their heads with the sole of his shoe, and then tossed them in the bushes, their headless bodies still fluttering.

In the aftermath of that long-ago shooting, with a temperature of 105 and rising, Joe had no choice but to go to the hospital. "I didn't want to be a cliché," he says ruefully about walking into a textbook rubout. "I thought I was a little too smart to be a cliché."

Sitting in the emergency room, he watched as a crash cart surrounded by nurses and physicians shot past him toward the outside courtyard, where some ambulances were parked.

Joe craned his neck to watch. "I don't know what happened out there," he thought to himself. "Must be bad."

Twenty seconds later, the ER team rushed back in, and asked the admitting nurse where the gunshot victim was.

The weary nurse pushed one of them to the side to clear her field of vision, then pointed to Joe. "He's there."

Joe stayed in the hospital long enough to get intravenous antibiotics and a fuzzy radiograph. As the surgeons prepared the operating room to remove the bullets, a reinvigorated Joe snuck out of his room and hopped into a waiting car with his only trusted friend, who arrived unsummoned with a change of clothes for him. Joe had him drop him off at his car.

The next step was obvious. Revenge.

But as Joe trolled the streets of his neighborhood, past the linen stores that sold ribbon-trimmed christening gowns and the Italian delis with provolones the size of fire hydrants in the windows, he thought about his family, and the chain reaction he might be igniting.

"I'm a pretty street-wise guy—I deserve what I get. Everybody makes their own bed, and puts themselves in those situations," Joe says. "But I'm not dragging other people into it. And I know if they can't get to me, they're going to get to someone I love or care about. So sometimes you have to swallow things that you don't want to."

Resigned, Joe headed back to his basement apartment. All he could think about was how and when his attackers would come, where he should shoot to defend himself, and how he should make an exit.

Hungover, cold, and racked with pain, he was so deep in thought that he did not notice another presence, one that shadowed him silently from one room to the next until, as he lowered himself into the chair, he felt the thud at his feet.

"I had nobody," he remembers thinking. "No friends I could trust anymore. But you know what I had? I had my dog"—a big Rottweiler named Blackjack.

His thoughts raced ahead. Blackjack could alert him to someone's presence long before he could sense it, and the dog's imposing bark would be a deterrent. "I thought, I'm pretty safe here because I have him. I never went to sleep that night, and the dog never did, either."

Long before Sally's videocassette ran out of tape, Joe had seen enough squirrels with mutilated faces, birds with twisted necks, and raccoons pacing obsessively in cold metal traps. It was time for a visit to this guy's neighborhood.

Sally gave him her tormentor's address, adding that the house number was superfluous: Once he was on the block, the house would announce itself.

She was right. Three flags flew in front—American, Confederate, and MIA/POW. A small herd of lawn signs had been staked in the ground warning against trespassing and lauding the National Rifle Association. "I am a bitter gun owner, and I vote," read one. Not exactly your average suburban homestead.

Joe and Big Ant pulled up on their Harleys, while Angel, G, and Bruce followed in cars.

They knocked on the front door, and a figure looked down at them from a second-floor window. He had a phone in one hand; his other hand was behind his back.

"We want to talk to you about some stuff," Joe called up to him.

"What stuff?"

"Come down," Joe said, "and we'll talk to you."

A few minutes later the man appeared at his front door.

"Stop—don't get any closer," he said, and Joe paused on the grass about ten feet from the door. The rest of the Rescue Ink guys were behind Joe and on the man's crumbling driveway.

Joe indicated there had been a lot of complaints about what had been happening with the animals. "And we're here to get your side of the story."

He asked if he could come into the house.

"No, you can't."

"Why not?"

"I don't want you to."

"Who are you talking to on the phone?"

"My lawyer."

"Tell him I said hello," Angel called over.

"Let me talk to him," said Joe, shouting out his cell phone number for the lawyer to call.

It was a deliberate decision on his part. "I wanted the crazy man to have my number," he says. "I'd rather have him focus his rage on somebody else than on those women. I've dealt with crazy people all my life, and it isn't the person that calls you on the phone that you worry about. The person you worry about will be hiding in the bushes when you come home."

Joe's cell phone rang.

"You're congregating in front of my client's house, and I'm putting you on warning you can't talk to him anymore," Joe remembers a very officious-sounding voice saying at the other end of the line.

"Who are you?" asked Joe, annoyed.

"I'm his lawyer."

"Well, I'm Joe Panz from Rescue Ink," he said back into the phone, spitting out every word like a cherry pit. "I answer to no one. So come down and try and make me do something."

Joe and the Rescue Ink guys stayed around for a while longer, talking to more neighbors. It was only women, it seemed, who had garnered the squirrel killer's attention.

But soon it became obvious that there was little left to do. They were at a stalemate. And Joe found himself dealing with a thought that for him was the most frustrating of all: the realization that to push things further at this point might imperil the very women he was seeking to protect.

Every day after the shooting, Joe got up, dressed himself with his usual care, and headed out the door, stopping before he turned the knob to compose himself. His goal was to be unruffled, unharmed, untouchable. Back straight, chest out, gaze unbroken. To show weakness, he knew, would bring the wolves. He was a pariah, to be sure, but he was never a rat, and as his body encased the bullets that remained inside him, so too did he wall off his anger. It happened, it was over, and that was that.

But Joe knew that Sally could never hide her fear—it was palpable, it was visceral, and, he believed, her animal-snuffing neighbor was feeding off it.

With his visit, he had agitated her tormentor, and he knew in his bones that once Rescue Ink left, he would act out again.

That night, Joe left Sally with the only thing he could: good advice.

"I'm not a liar. I am not going to give you a false sense of security," he said, encouraging her to keep up the precautions she was taking, such as calling a sympathetic neighbor to watch her enter her house whenever she came home after dark. "Don't go outside, lock your windows and doors. You don't know what this guy is capable of—he could be eating soup out of your skull next week. Just be very careful."

Joe also gave his number to Linda, the other neighbor who had an order of protection. She shared pictures of a possum, rabbits, and other dead animals that had materialized in the back of her flatbed truck and on her front lawn; her cat had also mysteriously disappeared. The next two cats she acquired were never let out of the house for fear they would meet a similar fate. She was also worried enough about the safety of her three dogs—a mastiff, a Jack Russell terrier, and a German shepherd—that she was moving four miles away.

"Trust me, I am a person with the biggest heart for animals, but there was nothing I could do—I had exhausted all my options with the police and the town," Linda says about relocating from the block where she was born and raised. "When Rescue Ink came, I thought, 'Wow, somebody cares.'"

But caring is not the same as doing. And that is what Joe finds so difficult. The in-your-face approach to animal abuse appears to have met its match with this case. All he can do for now is watch from afar. He keeps in constant contact with Sally by phone, and recently attended a small-claims court date with Linda, who was worried for her safety because she was testifying on behalf of a neighbor the man was suing.

"He has brief periods when he seems to go dormant, but then seems to get manic again, revs up, and gets agitated," wrote Sally recently in one of her many e-mail updates to Joe. "The more agitated he gets, the more he goes outside and puts out more and more birdseed, so we now also have rats coming. In the summer, the whole backyard smelled of dead animals from the ones he did not throw in our yards. It was reeking. At least when I see him getting agitated, I know to be very careful. There are always signs."

Joe recently came across a posting to Rescue Ink's MySpace page that struck a chord with him. It retold a Navajo legend about a grandfather who explained his spiritual struggles to his grandson.

"Two wolves live inside me," the old man explained. "One is good. He lives in peace and balance with the world, and he is full of joy and compassion. The other wolf is full of anger, ready to fight at the slightest offense. And in his blind rage he cannot think or change anything." All the time, the old man explained, the wolves were at battle within him, each one seeking to dominate. "Which one wins, Grandfather?" the boy asked intently. The grandfather smiled and replied, "The one I feed."

Today, Joe Panz is a businessman—and a Harley-riding

rescuer. He knows there is a time and a place, and that it is the job of law enforcement and the criminal-justice system to deal with Sally's neighbor. He only hopes nothing dire has to happen to finally get their attention. And in the meantime, he wrestles with the two wolves within.

8

Robert

Abusers Are Losers

Robert Misseri tells a story that has been circulating through his family for decades.

Growing up in Bensonhurst, an unavoidably Italian neighborhood in Brooklyn, Robert was always an animal lover. When he was nine or ten years old, "I used to knock on people's doors and ask if I could walk their dogs, which were usually chained outside all day," he remembers. "When other kids were stepping on praying mantises, I was bringing them home as pets."

On his regular walks through the neighborhood, the young Robert noticed a large mastiff who always seemed to be tied to a tree outside a social club. "People had to step off the sidewalk and onto the street to pass the club," which was the whole point of placing the dog in that spot in the first place, he says. But for some reason the dog didn't try to run off Robert, who would stop by and pet him despite the icy looks he got from the men playing cards inside the always occupied but eerily still social club.

One day, during a rainstorm that verged on sleet, Robert thought about the dog outside on the sidewalk without any shelter from the elements. "I went back and took the dog, and three hours later, two guys came to my house," he says. They had asked around the neighborhood, and "it was no secret that I would do anything to save an animal." When his mother pressed him, Robert led the irritated visitors to the boiler room.

"Kid, you should never steal," Robert recalls one of the wiseguys admonishing him as he untied the dog.

"And you should never leave your dog out in the rain," Robert replied.

According to Robert, that dog remained inside the club forever after.

As childhood anecdotes go, Robert's shows a degree of chutzpah that has been his calling card for much of his life. After all, it took more than a bit of nerve to envision a rescue group that would break all the rules, show that tough guys can have hearts of gold, and that a little testosterone introduced into an arena heretofore presided over by impassioned cat ladies wasn't such a bad thing.

"Men are absent from rescue, and I think we're gonna change that," Robert says of Rescue Ink. "I think men feel a little silly, like it's not cool or it's more of a woman's thing."

Robert brings an entrepreneurial spirit to Rescue Ink that's infused every business venture he has been involved in, whether it's buying and selling classic cars, opening a restaurant, or running a repair shop. "I was always a doer," explains Robert, describing how he put out food for stray neighborhood cats as an eleven-year-old.

While Robert is not always on every rescue, he is perpetually

Clara the bulldog before her abduction from the side-walk in front of an Upper West Side supermarket. *(Jessica Kurland)*

Clara's owner, Jessica Kurland, celebrates her dog's return with Big Ant and Batso (and G in the background). *(Jessica Kurland)*

Model Beth Ostrosky and then-fiancé Howard Stern pose with Joe Panz and Big Ant. *(Rescue Ink)*

Johnny O with Gracie, a pit bull who lived in a backyard with little socialization, and was eventually left at a kill shelter by her owners. *(Tony Trezza)*

I love Lucy: This brindle female with the white blaze is Johnny's first pit bull—but not his last. *(Rescue Ink)*

The cat whose ascent up a tree eventually prompted Johnny to call an arborist to intervene. *(Rescue Ink)*

Johnny's first attempts at reaching the gravity-defying feline by ladder just prompted the cat to retreat higher. *(Rescue Ink)*

This residence for a Rottweiler and a Great Dane mix was more like a condo than a mere doghouse. *(Rescue Ink)*

The finished product, awaiting its Rescue Ink decal—and its residents. *(Rescue Ink)*

Dolce the Rottweiler snoozes with two of Eric's miniature pinschers. *(Rescue Ink)*

Eric with Ann, the Maine resident who adopted his beloved Rottie, Dolce. *(Rescue Ink)*

Some of the many kittens removed from a house where the cat population had ballooned to almost 180 cats. *(Robert Helman)*

Kittens such as these were offered for adoption once they were spayed and neutered, treated by a vet, and socialized with ample human contact. *(Robert Helman)*

Des holds a baby kitten at the clubhouse. *(Rescue Ink)*

Big guy, small cat: Joe offers a study in contrasts. *(Tony Trezza)*

Like many cats from "the cat house," this one had extra digits on its front paws. *(Tony Trezza)*

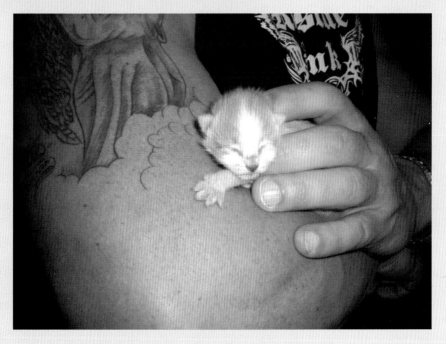

Joe and Big Ant flank Batso and his rescued pit-Lab mix, Inka. *(Rescue Ink)*

Batso's namesake car and his labor of love, the Bat's Revenge. *(Rescue Ink)*

When she's not lounging in classic cars, Inka spends most of her time gazing out from her perch at the front window. *(Rescue Ink)*

Batso developed a real fondness for Brownie, a longhair dachshund who has difficulty walking because of a back injury. *(Tony Trezza)*

Joe shares a contemplative moment with Bond, the pit bull–bullmastiff mix he rescued from a shelter—and, likely, euthanasia. *(Rescue Ink)*

Joe: a man and his Harley. *(Rescue Ink)*

Outside the home of a senior citizen whose neighbors accuse him of torturing, drowning, and dismembering animals. *(Tony Trezza)*

Robert with his rescued dog, Haley. *(Rescue Ink)*

Some of the outdoor cats that Robert feeds and shelters at his home. *(Rescue Ink)*

Robert horses around at the Sorvino family farm with animal activist Amanda, her father Paul, and Buttercup, a horse who was saved from slaughter. *(Rescue Ink)*

Old school met new school when Batso and Big Ant "tricked out" this once-battered ambulance and turned it into a pet emergency vehicle. *(Rescue Ink)*

This substantial sow and three piglets were just some of the porcines living at the home of an over-whelmed rescuer. Using a metal gate, Big Ant and Johnny held back the sow, who charged once she realized they were trying to crate and remove her babies. *(Rescue Ink)*

Big Ant with two American icons: his Harley and his pit bull, a female puppy named Butchie. *(Rescue Ink)*

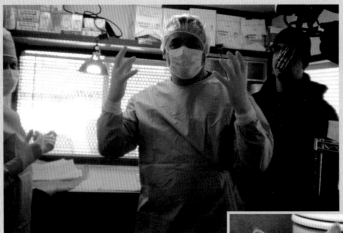

"Dr. Joe" suits up to witness his first cat neuter. *(Rescue Ink)*

This litter of kittens was raised in a bathroom at the Rescue Ink clubhouse. *(Rescue Ink)*

Plenty to go around: Bruce, Johnny, Joe, Ant, and Robert with some of the cats and kittens rescued from a house with as many as 180 resident felines. *(Tony Trezza)*

Des chats with a passerby at a cat-adoption event on the Upper West Side. *(Robert Helman)*

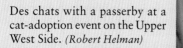

Curious Manhattanites stop to admire adoptable cats in a heated cage system that Des devised. *(Robert Helman)*

So what if his mother dresses him funny? Luigi the toothless Maltese is Mary's ever-present sidekick. *(Tony Trezza)*

Big Ant, Eric, and Junior with rescue dogs Marshall and Marcos at a local adoption event. *(Tony Trezza)*

Eric introduces a young friend to a Rottie mix named Brody. *(Tony Trezza)*

Ever versatile, Luigi does his impression of a muff as Bruce takes a rescue call. *(Tony Trezza)*

Whenever ex–police officer Angel Nieves is investigating a case at his computer, Cris the bichon frise supervises. *(Rescue Ink)*

Johnny O and friend Sugar, whom Rescue Ink gave to a little girl after she tearfully returned her own rescued poodle to the owner who had lost it. *(Rescue Ink)*

Rescue Ink protested against commercial dog breeders in the Amish countryside of Lancaster, Pennsylvania, during the Puppy Mill Awareness Day March in September 2008. *(Rescue Ink)*

G's pride and joy is his Suzuki Hayabusa, a hyper sport motorcycle. *(Rescue Ink)*

Spike is a Rottweiler–pit bull mix who spent a year of his life, maybe more, in a five-foot-by-five-foot pen. *(Rescue Ink)*

G soon persuaded Spike to get along with his gregarious Olde English bulldog, whose name is Boss. *(Rescue Ink)*

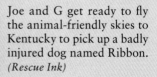

Joe and G get ready to fly the animal-friendly skies to Kentucky to pick up a badly injured dog named Ribbon. *(Rescue Ink)*

Emaciated and scarred, Ribbon was likely a bait dog, used to build aggression and "gameness" in fighting dogs. *(Rescue Ink)*

Ribbon's namesake: the streamers of skin that framed his face were all that was left of his ears. *(Rescue Ink)*

G and Joe pick up Ribbon from the veterinarian who fostered him for two weeks. *(Rescue Ink)*

Touchdown! The trio arrives in New York in the middle of the night. *(Rescue Ink)*

Meeting at the clubhouse soon after the dog's arrival, the guys voted to rename him Rebel, a nod to his Southern roots.
(Tony Trezza)

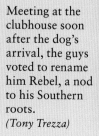

Rescue Ink poses in front of the clubhouse, with Big Ant's classic car adding a retro touch. *(Joe Laronga)*

Striking a pose at Rockabilly Barbers in East Northport. *(Tony Trezza)*

behind the scenes, networking with local and national groups, trying to organize spay-and-neuter programs, and spreading the Rescue Ink message across the country, and beyond national borders to the rest of the world.

When Robert was eighteen years old, he moved to Long Island, where he met "the toughest cat I ever knew in my life." Mr. McNasty, as Robert dubbed him, started hanging around the house after Robert began feeding him. One day the cat arrived for his chow with his back leg dragging. It looked as if he had been hit by a car. Robert took him to the vet, only to find that he was riddled with BBs. Robert had the vet go ahead with the $1,100 surgery, paying off the bill in increments. And when he married five years later at age twenty-three and moved with his wife to their first home, Mr. McNasty accompanied them, cantankerous and obstinate to the end.

Today, Robert, forty, helps run his family's corporate catering business in Manhattan. He still has a pronounced soft spot for cats, and fosters kittens occasionally. "The reason I have such a focus on cats is, I can walk for a hundred blocks and never see a stray dog," he says, "but I can find a hundred cats. They are the bigger problem"—in the Northeast, at least. For the last three or four years, Robert has helped caretakers manage about twenty feral-cat colonies on Long Island by providing food and often shelters made of thirty-gallon Rubbermaid containers insulated with foam board and topped with tarp.

Kerry Keegan of Babylon says Robert helped him get help to trap and relocate more than two dozen cats from a site where there was evidence that the innocent creatures were being used for animal sacrifice in religious rituals. "Trapped and bludgeoned cats were placed on our feeding stations, and my wife found an eviscerated kitten's body between two candles," continues Kerry, who says no other group responded to his pleas for help and resources.

On his own property Robert feeds eight outdoor feral cats, and has one indoor cat of his own that was left at his mother's doorstep, half starved. He'd been declawed, which meant he would have had a very difficult, if not impossible, time surviving outdoors without any claws with which to defend himself. So Robert brought the cat into the house, despite the fact that he's allergic and has a dog, a four-year-old Lab-shepherd mix named Haley, also a rescue, who's not friendly with cats.

To hear Rob tell it, he's a sucker for a sob story. Take the example of the woman who came to buy a car from him and then told him about the horse she could no longer afford to keep. "I bought the horse, paid $700 for him, and then she was a couple months' arrears on his board, which was $300 a month," Robert says. The sixteen-year-old horse was half blind, and needed new shoes and a special diet. "I was the biggest laughingstock of the stable," he says. Sleeper, as Robert called him because every time he visited the horse was snoozing, lived for only another six months.

Before he got involved with creating Rescue Ink, Robert used to volunteer at animal shelters. "I stopped volunteering because it was hard on me, it was really affecting me," he says. "I was getting emotionally attached. In my mind, I had to keep believing they were all adopted." When that lie became impossible to believe, it was "out of sight, out of mind"—he stopped going to the shelters.

And that perhaps is the greatest unspoken truth about rescue. More than the anger and frustration at seeing animals discarded like fast-food wrappers, more than the sadness at seeing dogs that are starved or ripped up in dogfighting "practice," the most dangerous side effect in rescue is weariness.

"People get burned out in rescue," Robert says. "It's a burden on their families, and it wears them out. Financially, too. But some days at the end of a day of rescue, whether you're broke or not, you feel like a million bucks."

With a group like Rescue Ink, the burden is shared, shouldered by guys who don't take no for an answer, who'd rather take a tire iron to the gut than walk away from an abused or ill-treated animal. While he grew up in some of the same neighborhoods as the other guys, and met them over the years at classic-car shows, Robert doesn't look like any of them at first glance. But if there is one long stretch of common ground, it's the belief that as a group they can do far more good than any one of them acting alone.

The bald eagle may be the official emblem of the United States, but there is an animal that resonates even more deeply with Americans, one that represents the fierce independence and freedom of the Old West, the boundlessness of our national landscape.

For all his nobility and iconic stature, however, the horse has not always fared well at the hands of humans in this country. Abuse of draft horses in New York City led to the formation of the American Society for the Prevention of Cruelty to Animals in the 1860s; its gentleman-founder, Henry Bergh, in top hat and spats, would stop drivers he saw beating their animals, thus earning his nickname, "The Great Meddler." A century later, a new menopause drug called Premarin (a truncation of "pregnant mare urine") created generations of enslaved pregnant mares, tethered in narrow stalls for six months or more and attached to a urine-collection apparatus that dramatically restricted their movement.

Today, horse slaughter is technically legal in the United States, though state legislatures have been effective in stopping it at the municipal level. The three foreign-owned horse slaughter plants in the country were shuttered in 2007: Two in Texas closed when that state enforced a 1959 law banning the sale of horse meat for human consumption, and one in Ohio ceased operations when that state passed a law banning horse slaughter. Until the closure of those slaughterhouses, each year some 90,000 horses used for thoroughbred racing, draft work, or just pleasure riding were slaughtered on American soil.

While the slaughterhouses are now gone, the demand for their product is not: Horse meat is considered a delicacy in many countries, including France, Belgium, and Japan, where it is called *sakuraniku* ("cherry blossom meat") and is consumed raw. To satisfy this overseas appetite for horseflesh, thousands of unwanted American horses are still sent across the border to Mexican and Canadian slaughterhouses. Transported in double-decker trailers intended for cattle, the horses are sometimes injured and trampled when they arrive at their destination. Investigators from the Humane Society of the United States (HSUS) have documented the inhumane killing methods in Mexican slaughterhouses, which include stabbing the spine with a short knife, leaving the animals paralyzed and sometimes still conscious when their throats are slit. According to the HSUS, more than 86,000 horses were sent across U.S. borders to slaughter in Canada or Mexico in 2008, a larger number than in 2007.

There is, thankfully, reform afoot. In early 2009, the newly created Congressional Animal Protection Caucus announced that addressing horse slaughter was high on its agenda. And a proposed law, the Prevention of Equine Cruelty Act (H.R. 503), seeks to prohibit this back-door transport of horses to Mexico and Canada to be slaughtered for consumption by humans.

Late in 2008, Robert got a phone call from Amanda Sorvino, an impassioned animal rescuer living in Pennsylvania. Two of Amanda's family members have a pretty high profile: Her father is the rugged actor Paul Sorvino, famous for playing law-enforcement and gangster types on film and television, and her sister is Academy Award–winning actress Mira Sorvino.

Several years ago Amanda began to foster and rehabilitate dogs on her father's Poconos compound, where she lived as well. With a wink at her father's role as brooding mobster Paul Cicero in the 1990 film *Goodfellas*, she named the rescue operation "Dogfellas." With Amish country about a hundred miles to the southwest, Amanda became focused on the state's puppy-mill problem.

It was perhaps inevitable, then, that Amanda would began to turn her attention to other animals as well, particularly horses, which she admired for their majestic bearing and deeply spiritual nature. Amanda told Robert that she had been investigating a slaughterhouse that, in addition to rendering cows, also killed horses—not for human consumption, but to feed zoo animals.

"I had no idea that it was legal in this country to slaughter horses to feed to lions and tigers in zoos. We're in the Dark

Ages when it comes to protecting animals under the law," says Robert, who got an education on the subject from Amanda. She had her own concerns about how humanely the animals were being slaughtered at the facility, and had decided to go undercover to learn more, as well as to save as many horses as she could from being turned into lunch for captive cheetahs. "This case was the first time I understood what was going on with horses in America," Robert says.

Theatricality in her blood, Amanda created an alter ego for herself—Aspen Wrigley, a pro-slaughter horsewoman who befriended the slaughterhouse manager at local rodeos and horse events. Soon, she says, she was visiting the slaughterhouse and trying to persuade the manager that she could get a good price for the horses from affluent parents who wanted to use the creatures as therapy animals for their autistic or emotionally troubled children. She also suggested that the horses could be sold for research. The man would still get his price—and save himself the trouble of slaughtering the horses. What he didn't know is that she would then whisk the horses off to her rescue, the newly created Gray Dapple Thoroughbred Assistance Program.

"Amanda called and said she no longer felt comfortable meeting with the guy alone," Robert remembers. "She called everyone under the sun." No one responded except Rescue Ink.

Robert contacted Mark Jurnove, an animal advocate who investigates abuse, especially of livestock and exotics, and got him to agree to accompany Amanda in the guise of her elderly uncle. Robert also dispatched Eric to accompany them to the slaughter facility.

Mark snapped pictures of three cows with bullet wounds—none of them in the head—lying in their own blood, clearly still alive. Federal law requires that animals be slaughtered humanely, with one bullet to the head.

"Slaughter has to be done in a prescribed fashion, and in a humane way, by rendering these animals quickly," says Stu Goldman, a special investigations agent for the Monmouth County, New Jersey, SPCA. "They are also not supposed to be slaughtered in the presence of other animals, because this creates stress and anxiety. It's torturous and tormenting to a certain degree to watch your fellow animal die, especially for herd animals such as horses and cows," which are so finely attuned to each other's mental state.

Eric vividly remembers that visit to what he calls the "chop shop." It was everything he could do to keep from pounding the guy into the ground. "We were at the horse corral, and one of the horses had a bad hoof," Eric says. "The guy said, 'That one might be good for this disabled kid that needs a horse,' and then he kicked the horse in the leg to show how messed up it was. Then he said, 'See that one out there?'" Eric continues. "He said, 'That one's name is Cunt, and she's going to get a bullet in the head tomorrow.'"

Eric listened as Amanda talked to the man, urging him to fatten up the horses so they could be candidates for therapy horses and research prospects. "Amanda said, 'I can get three thousand dollars for some of these horses,'" Eric remembers. "'But you gotta beef them up.'"

Sensing that her undercover identity was soon to be blown, Amanda says she later went to the slaughterhouse when the manager was away on a trip and persuaded an employee to sell her eight of the horses headed for slaughter. To augment the funds that Amanda's father, Paul, provided to rescue the horses, Rescue Ink supplied her with money for blankets and food for the slaughterhouse survivors. "I asked everyone for help," Amanda says, "but Robert and Rescue Ink were the only ones who answered."

For that little band of horses, at least, happy endings were fated. Five were sent to the Midwest to be fostered with a friend of Amanda's who has dozens of acres of pastureland, until they are able to be adopted.

The only one who will probably never leave is Scotchy, a five-year-old Belgian horse who had plowed fields on an Amish farm. He arrived blind in one eye and lost sight in the other, Amanda was told, as a result of being struck by a blunt object at the slaughterhouse.

An infection had developed in the injured eye, and Amanda took Scotchy to an equine vet who immediately hospitalized him and removed the eye. Now totally blind, Scotchy will likely live out his life out west or at Gray Dapple, with Amanda as his savior and final owner.

Three of the rescue horses remained with Amanda at Gray Dapple. One is Buttercup. On her Web site, Amanda has photos of the former racehorse at the slaughterhouse, with open sores on her legs and ankles. Once Buttercup gains some weight, Amanda hopes to adopt her out as a children's riding horse.

The other horse, Franky's Girl, is completely lame and will be adoptable only as a "pasture pal."

And the third, twenty-four-year-old Midnight Glitter, was too weak to make a recovery and died while at the Sorvinos'. He was buried on the farm, his grave covered with a shiny silver wreath.

As for the slaughterhouse, Amanda is hopeful that law enforcement will look into slaughter practices there and determine if wrongdoing has occurred. Until then, she and Robert take satisfaction in knowing that they played some part in saving a few good horses from a very bad end.

Rescue Ink's catchphrase is that the group has an "in-your-face approach" to animal abuse and neglect. To be sure, doing "door knocks" at the homes of abusers is the bread and butter of this group.

For his part, Robert often takes a wider view of the impact the group can have on the local rescue community. His end-of-the-rainbow list of projects includes an animal food bank for owners who cannot afford quality kibble or canned food for their pets. He'd also like to see Rescue Ink's influence spread to places like Puerto Rico, where packs of feral dogs are as omnipresent as cat colonies here in the States.

Another of Robert's brainstorms is a fully equipped animal ambulance that could serve economically challenged communities whose pet owners cannot afford emergency veterinary care. He came up with the idea when he got a call from an elderly woman on a fixed income in Astoria, Queens, whose dog had broken its leg, and she had no way to get it to a vet. Robert drove to the woman's home, carried the elderly shepherd mix out, and had it treated. "Animals suffer when their owners cannot afford proper medical care," Robert says of the ambitious ambulance project. "There is no 911 for cats and dogs."

The PETTmobile—which stands for "primary emergency transfer and treatment"—was donated to Rescue Ink by Robert's brother, and has seen better days. It needed a new front bumper, and corroded parts of the body had to be cut out and repaired. As for the diesel engine, the one thing that can be said in its favor is that it runs. "The ambulance needs an ambulance," notes Big Ant wryly.

Along with Batso, Big Ant has taken on the challenge of "pimping" this very institutional-looking ride, which required an industrial-strength tow truck to schlep it to a car shop way out in Bohemia, a Suffolk County community that, despite its utopian name, has its share of industrial parks. Though the two men have a similar vision for the hulking truck, their techniques have a significant generation gap, with Batso taking a decidedly old-school approach: When they removed the medical decals on the side of the ambulance, Batso used a heat gun and scraper, the way he's done it for sixty years. Big Ant used a rubber grinder, which removed the decals in seconds instead of minutes, leaving the paint job underneath untouched.

It would be weeks or months before the ambulance hit the road with its all-black paint job and side-licking red flames. But Big Ant couldn't resist taking it for a test drive.

Emergency response is a subject that resonates for Robert, who was a responder on September 11. "When I heard about the towers, I filled one of our catering vans with water bottles and drove downtown," he says. "We started handing out water bottles outside the red zone to the people passing by, who were covered in dust and soot." The next day, it became apparent that the firemen, police, and other disaster personnel at the site needed to be fed. Along with a newly met friend from out of state, Robert created a Ground Zero food-service station on John Street, with a forty-foot tent from the Army Corps of Engineers, cooking hundreds of meals a day, from hamburgers and hot dogs to chicken and vegetables. When he shut that down after a month and a half, he continued to serve free breakfast, lunch, and dinner to the local firehouses near his Midtown office, all of which had lost men in the collapsing Twin Towers. Robert has a thick file of proclamations from various entities thanking him for his work during those dark days, from New York governor George Pataki to the Red Cross.

Rescue Ink and the guys have come a long way since they started a little more than two years ago with not much more than a handful of local tough guys and a handful of cases. Back then, the guys had to rent a van whenever they traveled anywhere as a group. And before there was Bruce or Mary to help run the back office, Robert took the calls, coordinated the media inquiries, and piloted the "vision thing" simultaneously.

Today, Rescue Ink still operates pretty much as a large but dysfunctional family. Sometimes it gets loud, sometimes it gets exuberant, but at the end of the day, things work out.

"I want to create a social taboo about abusing animals," says Robert, who has gotten e-mails from as far away as Ireland and Israel saying that Rescue Ink has helped change social views on animal rescue.

Today Long Island, tomorrow the world.

9

Big Ant

Bacon's Revenge

𝕿he mama pigs were pissed.

Big Ant surveyed the two oinkers in the pigpen. If he had to guess, the larger one was five hundred pounds, about double the size she should have been thanks to too-generous rations. Dolly and Matilda—it was unclear which was which—squealed in equal parts anger and frustration as he and Johnny surveyed their pen and tried to determine the best way to capture their three piglets.

It was probably no consolation to the porcine matriarchs, but Rescue Ink was not called to this residence solely for pig wrangling. The owner of the property was a rescuer gone amok. Bighearted and perhaps too ambitious, the elderly caretaker had more animals than she could handle. Inside her house was a kind of animal Bizarro World: dozens of birds, from parakeets to lovebirds to canaries, flew around the rooms, alighting on chandeliers and sofa backs, while just as many cats paced in bird cages. Rescuers were on hand to transport all the animals to foster homes—they just needed a hand corralling them.

A local pig rescuer—yes, there is such a thing—called Rescue Ink to the scene to help capture the piglets she hoped to find homes for. She hadn't appreciated the guys ordering bacon at their requisite diner stop before arriving, but novice pig catchers need their sustenance, after all.

Farm animals are nothing new to Big Ant, whose oxymoronic name is self-explanatory: he's big, and his name is Anthony. His Italian-immigrant parents kept chickens and goats in the backyard of their Queens home in a neighborhood not far from where Joe Panz grew up. In this vista of concrete, the only open stretch of land was the nearby racetrack. Still, Big Ant's parents insisted on maintaining their inverted, borough-bred version of *Green Acres*.

"People going to catch the train in the morning would walk by and yell, 'You're in Queens, New York! This ain't upstate!'" says Big Ant, now thirty-nine, remembering the family of ducklings that used to follow him around the yard. "But to us it was like, 'Hey, how you doin'?'" a catchall phrase Ant uses when he's looking to break the tension, create a distraction, acknowledge an impasse.

Big Ant's livestock experience really started on his uncle's farm just outside of Naples, Italy. For as long as he can remember, his parents, kids in tow, crisscrossed the Atlantic periodically, visiting family in Italy for month-long stretches, then returning to New York to seek the prosperity that had eluded them in the first few years they spent there.

The farm near Naples had an Old MacDonald assortment of cows, chickens, and, yes, pigs. Every house had a few dogs who earned their keep by herding and tending the sheep, whose milk made delicious, pungent cheese. Big Ant remembers the difficulties involved with some of the cows during calving, and how the men of the family would tie a rope to the hooves of the breech baby, line up outside the stall, and with orchestrated heave-hos pull it out rudely into the awaiting world.

Technology was pretty much nonexistent: Big Ant's grandmother didn't have an indoor toilet or a stove, and all the food was cooked in the fireplace. The family washed their clothes in the communal *fontana*, where the women shared the gossip of the day over their washboards. But sustenance was never far away. Corn, apples, tomatoes, and grapes all waited to be plucked from nearby fields; the day's milk was squirted into a bucket before dawn. "I used to grab an egg from the chickens in the morning, crack the whole top off it, sprinkle some sugar on top, and eat it raw," Ant remembers. "It was a nice brown egg, a real one, no supermarket thing. I saw the guy who laid it."

As bucolic as Big Ant's life was on that farm near Naples, across the ocean in the United States he and his family faced real adversity in the Brooklyn tenement where they started their immigrant experience.

East New York had once been a predominantly Italian neighborhood, populated by men with callused hands who worked construction and masonry jobs, and by women who scrubbed their stoops with boiling water until they shone.

But by the time Big Ant's family arrived on Eastern Parkway and Pennsylvania Avenue, where the Number 3 train rattled and screeched overhead, the neighborhood had changed, and not for the better. One of his earliest memories is watching from his playpen as a group of men broke into the family apartment, a relatively regular occurrence. As four-year-old Anthony watched, the men flipped over furniture and turned drawers upside down. His mother, who had gone to the basement to drop off the laundry and figured her preschool son would be safer locked in the apartment, encountered the fleeing men on the stairs, where they almost knocked her over. Then, as she did countless times, his mother cried, mourning the impoverished but safer life she had left in Italy.

The break-in "was my first confrontation with life," shrugs Big Ant matter-of-factly. "I think it just made me stronger," he says. "It made me who I am."

School was hit-and-miss for Big Ant: He started kindergarten speaking only Italian, and his family's frequent trips abroad meant he missed a lot of school. In third grade, his mother became ill, and he lost big chunks of time staying home to take care of her.

By then, his family had moved to the animal-friendly house in Queens, and though the neighborhood was a little better, it was still tough. Big Ant remembers being at a teenage cousin's house while all the adults were at a wedding when they heard a window break and someone land with a thump on the floor. Quickly, quietly, he helped herd the smaller children into a bathroom, where they listened in silence as the men ran back and forth in the house, looting and ransacking.

"I wasn't worried—I'd been through this already," Big Ant says. In Brooklyn, the break-ins had been so frequent that his father had siphoned all his whiskey into mason jars and replaced it with tea, as the liquor bottles were the first thing the thieves pocketed.

In that tense bathroom, crowded with children, "I kept telling them, 'No noise, no noise,' and everybody was OK" with keeping quiet, Big Ant remembers.

Then one of the robbers started turning the doorknob. "Everybody lost it," Big Ant says of his cousins, who began to scream and howl. "But I knew what to do. I was holding the doorknob. I was thinking, They ain't coming in."

To this day, he can see that doorknob turning and turning. And then, just as it did that night, in his memory it stops, and the house is still, and he and his cousins are safe. For that moment, at least.

Across the street from the woman with the caged cats and the portly pigs was a young man whose pit bull had just had a litter. Rumor had it that he was a gang member. The guy was friendly enough—and with a pregnant wife of his own, he was a little overwhelmed with the furry arrivals. Big Ant remembers, "We said, we don't give a fuck who you are, we want to take those puppies and give them a good home."

Rescue Ink has rescued all kinds of animals—piranhas and horses, ducks and turtles. But everyone has his weakness, and with this crew it's dogs, specifically pit bulls. "They're the best dogs there are out there," says Ant, who rescued a pit bull puppy of his own from a Queens car dealer who needed to get rid of some of the dogs on his lot. Her name is Butchie, and she is a wriggling mass of love and attention.

"It's just unbelievable how they listen to you," Ant says. "Pit bulls are not just dogs—they're like humans. And it's such a shame that they get a bad rap."

As Ant and Johnny O busied themselves with the pigs, G, Batso, and a couple of the other Rescue Ink guys negotiated the handover of the puppies. Eventually, the young man gave them three of the four. Given that the pigs were still charging anyone who approached their pen, getting a gangbanger to hand over his precious pups would prove to be the easiest rescue of the day.

Big Ant and Johnny concluded that the only way to capture the pink piglets, which were as big as full-grown pit bulls themselves, was to keep their angry mothers at bay. The rescue woman had her two teenage sons cornered and held one of the pigs back with an iron-rail fence, while on the opposite side of the pen, Big Ant and Johnny did the same with the other sow.

The rescue lady stayed in the center of the enclosure, trying to herd the piglets into large dog crates. When the first piglet ran into the molded-plastic crate and the wire door shut behind him, he let out a panicked squeal. Enraged and concerned for her baby's safety, Johnny and Ant's pig began to hurl herself at the metal gate.

Bam. Bam. Bam.

Big Ant strained to hold the metal barrier in place, but the pig persisted.

Bam. Bam. BAM.

This was going to be a long day.

The case of the lady with the ill-tempered pigs was a walk in the park compared to the hoarding case that Rescue Ink was called in to help with in June 2008.

Rescue Ink has a friendly relationship with the Nassau County Society for the Prevention of Cruelty to Animals, and the humane group asked Rescue Ink to assist them in an eviction case of two elderly brothers in Nassau County. The two men had an ancient, sickly shepherd mix, twenty-five cats—and no litter boxes.

"When we got there, one of the new SPCA guys was there, and he went in with us," says Big Ant. The feces on the floor were about an inch thick—once the human and animal residents left, the building would unquestionably have to be torn down. "That guy lasted two minutes, and came out throwing up."

A cameraman from a local news channel made a noble attempt as well, but he soon left retching, too.

But Joe, G, Johnny, Batso, Big Ant, and Des didn't have the luxury of calling it quits: It's not Rescue Ink's style to back down from a challenge, no matter how disgusting said challenge may be. Inside the house, cats were living in the walls, inside mattresses. Scratches from the cats were that much more dangerous because the cats' nails were encrusted in their own feces from the buildup underfoot.

"How you doin', all right?" Big Ant asked the two men, not expecting an answer. He pointed to the shards of porcelain littering the kitchen floor. "What's all this?"

"My brother likes to break plates over his head," explained the more coherent of the two siblings.

"Didn't you ever hear of paper plates?" deadpanned Big Ant.

Wearing thick gloves to protect against bites and scratches, the Rescue Ink guys used restraint poles to capture the skittish cats. Unlike dogs, which are more substantial and can be grabbed around the neck with the mechanism, cats are more delicate, and the loop must close in under their arms, sort of like a sling.

Animal hoarding, which used to be called by the more benign term "collecting," has not been studied extensively, and isn't formally designated as a psychological illness. But in a 2006 study, Gary J. Patronek, VMD, PhD, vice president for animal welfare and new program development at the Animal Rescue League of Boston, posited that at least three thousand cases of animal hoarding occur in the United States each year, involving a minimum of 250,000 animals, with many others likely going unreported.

Hoarding is on the increase, Patronek says, in large part because of the democratization of the animal-rescue world. "Twenty years ago, animal rescue was dominated by large mainstream organizations. There was no Internet, no grass-roots connection, and the idea of 'no kill,' however one defines that, wasn't something that existed," he says. "That all changed in the mid-1990s in a major way," as mom-and-pop animal rescue groups and privately run sanctuaries mushroomed. This grassroots empowerment undoubtedly saved the lives of many animals, "but it also opened up animal rescue to individuals who had no business doing it."

Hoarders tend to be older, single, and female, and had relatively unstable childhoods in which animals represented sources of love and consistency they didn't receive from parents or caretakers. A 1999 study by Patronek found that more than 80 percent of hoarders also stockpile inanimate objects relating to their rescue activity, like food cans, litter pans, and newspapers. And 60 percent, even after their animals were rescued or removed, just began accumulating animals again.

Despite the hoarders' assertions that they loved their animals deeply, treated them as surrogate children, and considered other people to be less competent in caring for them, 80 percent of cases in the study cited sick or dead animals. Though it is presumably not intentional, such neglect is still a form of animal abuse.

Patronek divides hoarders into at least three types. The mildest is the "overwhelmed caregiver," who is often aware to some degree of the severity of the situation and recognizes that the animals may be getting substandard care. In these cases, the animals are usually not as actively acquired—the hoarder may not visit animal shelters for new additions but rather agree to a friend's request to foster yet another animal, and another, and another—and often a dramatic life change such as a death or divorce triggers the crisis.

The next type is the "rescuer," who more actively acquires animals under the banner of rescue but rarely adopts them out to others, because of a belief that no one else could care for them as well. Unlike the overwhelmed caretaker, who often considers the animals a part of the family, the rescuer is less likely to live with the animals as companions. Often the animals live outside or in separate quarters from the hoarder's living area.

The last group Patronek describes is the "exploiter," who, as the name suggests, is in severe denial, and will rebuff offers of help and downsizing. With a tendency toward sociopathic behavior and an inability to empathize with humans or animals, these individuals are described as lacking in remorse, superficially charming and charismatic, and hugely manipulative.

But Big Ant and the guys in the crap-caked Nassau County house weren't thinking much about labels. One by one they removed the cats, put them in carriers, and loaded them into their vehicle. Once the twenty-five cats were crated safely in the van, they started the forty-mile ride east to Save-a-Pet, where the cats would receive veterinary care, be spayed and neutered, and hopefully, find new homes.

Twenty-five cats became twenty-nine when, en route, a heavily pregnant cat decided to have her kittens while zooming along the Long Island Expressway.

By the time the third piglet had been crated, the larger of the mother pigs had had enough. She was too strong for Johnny and Big Ant combined. Banging and straining against the metal gate, she finally prevailed and broke through.

"I knew a lot about farm animals before, but the one thing I learned that day was that pigs bite," Big Ant says solemnly, recalling the sow's slashing teeth as he and Johnny O held her back with the gate.

Running as fast as they could, Johnny and Big Ant jumped over the sides of the pen as the enraged pig nipped at their heels. Once they were out of range, she turned her attention to the middle of the pen, where the lady rescuer had just lifted the last crated piglet out of the pen. Now trapped by the sow, who loomed between her and the gate, the woman climbed on top of the one empty crate left in the pen.

The sow looked up at the lady perched on this strange beige box in the middle of her pen.

The pig had a plan.

Big Ant started getting interested in cars way back in his Brooklyn days. There's a photo of him as a five-year-old hanging out in his father's yellow-and-black 1970 Maverick.

"I fell in love," he says simply of his passion.

At ten years old Anthony built a makeshift car out of scrap parts. "Everyone was like, 'Cool car!'" Big Ant remembers with pride. "I was like, 'I built this sucker!'" He neglected, however, to put in any brakes, and his maiden voyage ended in a rendezvous with a fence and a few stitches.

By fourteen, Big Ant had acquired a real car. He started with the shell of a 1969 GTO that he slowly brought back to life on weekends with the help of friends who dropped in. His plan was to have the GTO finished by the time he was eligible for his driver's permit. He did. And it was fast. He quickly learned about the remote stretches of city blacktop like Fountain Avenue, near the dumps in Brooklyn, where drag racing thrived.

Soon Big Ant joined the biker world. Not only did he love motorcycles, he loved the solidarity and sense of identity among their riders, which more than made up for the danger that came along with riding them. Though he had a series of motorcycles in his teens, it wasn't until his twenties that he got the ultimate expression of chrome and horsepower: a Harley. He was riding a chopper long before it was stylish. But the bike wasn't a fashion accessory: It was a way of life.

And so, to some degree, was the ever-present threat of violence. "I've been having guns put into my face forever," says Big Ant almost wearily. The first time, he was nine or so, and four eighteen-year-olds accosted him and a friend, whose jacket they wanted.

"One of the guys jammed a gun in my face, and I'm thinking to myself, Why do I have to get a gun in my face when they want *his* jacket?" says Big Ant, who has a knack for getting extra helpings of danger even when he doesn't ask for them.

Satisfied with their loot, the laughing men had turned to leave when Ant shouted out a question: "Why didn't you just beat us up?"

One of the guys looked at him with a puzzled expression, hesitated, then kept going. "He was a coward," Big Ant says in disgust. "And that's what he heard"—calling him what he was, a coward—in the question from a boy half his age.

"I've had a million other incidents" since that time as a frightened nine-year-old with a gun pressed to his face, Big Ant says. But now, instead of fear, he feels an odd familiarity. "After living through incidents like that, nothing shocks me anymore."

In this world of loud bikes and patch-covered leather jackets, secret covenants, and strict expectations of loyalty, Big Ant found a fraternity of urban warriors whose ideological lineage, he says, stretches back through history. "The world hasn't really changed. You had your Vikings, your gladiators, your cowboys, and you got your bikers. These guys are men," Big Ant says. "They took me in, and they seen that I was a man also."

Later on, when Rescue Ink formed, with Big Ant as one of the founding members, that emphasis on self-reliance and strength from within continued. If there is one thing that the Rescue Ink guys believe to be just as vital as air and food and water, it is respect. Without the capacity to hold your head up, you might as well be dead. Big Ant is a jovial, joke-cracking, and easygoing guy. But once that line of respect has been crossed or ignored, like many of his Rescue Ink colleagues, he transforms in an instant, the air around him crackling with intensity.

"My biggest fear is being an ordinary joe," Big Ant admits. "Sometimes I'll sit and watch a guy in a nice suit ordering a coffee on his way to his office job. On the weekend he might do something with his pals, and I'm sure he's happy. But to me, that's not life. If you can't make a mark in this world, what do you got?"

When he was twenty-eight, Big Ant found himself in a situation with an outcome that threatened to be far worse than ordinary.

Because of circumstances he'd rather not discuss (the Rescue Ink guys reserve the right to edit their life stories, and who's going to argue?), Big Ant woke up one morning to find himself paralyzed from the waist down. No matter how much he tried to move them, his legs refused to work. Using his arms, he dragged himself down the stairs, down the driveway, and, palms raw and bleeding, met a friend at the curb—he refused to call an ambulance.

At the hospital before the operation, the surgeon stopped to talk to Big Ant.

"Listen," Ant remembers the surgeon saying. "I'll do whatever I can." The words, with their implication of permanent immobility, sounded like a death sentence to Big Ant.

"You gotta fucking kill me then," Big Ant responded as the dread grew in him. Death to him would have been a better option than a lifetime of helplessness.

The surgery went as well as could be expected, leaving him with a long gash that travels up his back from the base of his spine. Even after the surgery, the doctors didn't have any definite answers about whether he would walk again.

A few days later, a hospital staffer stopped in at Big Ant's room with a clutch of brochures in his hand.

"How you doin', all right?" Big Ant asked, taking the proffered papers. "What's this?"

"They're for wheelchairs," the man answered, pulling up a chair. "Listen, it's an adjustment you're going to be going through, and we want to get you the most comfortable chair, because you're going to be in it for the rest of your life."

Big Ant ushered the man out with more than a few choice words.

After a month-long hospitalization, Big Ant went to a rehab hospital. His girlfriend visited almost every night with his dog, Shop—named for the dog's ever-present status at the auto-body shop where Big Ant worked.

One night, he heard the sound of motorcycles roaring into the parking lot beneath his window. Dozens upon dozens of men on Harleys streamed into the lot, filling it entirely. Soon they were crowding his room, bearing gifts. Some of the more impromptu ones were borrowed from nearby patients. "I was like, this says, 'Get better, Harry,'" Big Ant remembers with a laugh.

After a month, Big Ant was able to stand, however briefly and unsteadily. What motivated him was part anger, part determination, part sheer will that he would hold back whatever was on the other side of that ominously turning doorknob from his boyhood. "There were people in my therapy with less problems than I had," he says, "and I was like, fuck you, don't pity me, because I'm gonna walk out of here."

Big Ant was sent home, and continued to work on regaining control of his legs at an outpatient therapy facility. At one point he grew complacent and took to using the wheelchair around the house because it was easier than the slow, shaky steps he was taking.

Again, his friends bolstered him: They stole his wheelchair.

"I never saw it again," says Big Ant. And soon, after more months of hard work, he never needed it again, either.

The pig rescuer was balanced on top of the empty crate, like a strange bird on a cliff in the middle of a raging ocean.

Below her, the determined sow charged into the crate.

"Grab my hand!" Big Ant yelled, reaching over the fence into the enclosure.

The woman ignored him and concentrated on keeping her balance.

The pig came back and broadsided the crate again, this time so hard that the woman wobbled and dropped to her knees on top of the crate, which was about as big as a bath mat.

"Here! My hand—take it!" Anthony shouted again. This time the woman listened, and reached out to grab his arm.

With every ounce of strength he had, Anthony flipped the woman through the air, like a shotput, and she landed outside the pen.

"How you doin', all right?" Big Ant asked, extending his hand to help her off the ground.

Behind him, five hundred pounds of swine snorted in frustrated fury.

10

Herding Cats

Catch Us If You Can

$\mathcal{A}$ meeting at the clubhouse had been called to discuss the cat house—specifically, how Rescue Ink was going to handle its return visit to the Center Moriches house from which the homeowner, and her estimated 180 cats, were due to be evicted in a few short months.

"I have a vet," began Des earnestly.

"I have a Mustang," Big Ant deadpanned.

The Corvette joke got a couple of snickers, but the room soon grew quiet as Des explained the logistics involved in processing so many cats. This wasn't just going to be any old day of cat-slinging, and the closest Rescue Ink had come to a rescue of this magnitude was removing a couple of dozen cats from that studio apartment in Nassau County. For the Center Moriches case, Des had created detailed, numbered intake forms to record and organize vital information, ranging from the cat's estimated age and gender to its weight and potential medical issues. Each form had a number that corresponded to database software he used to track the sheltering, medical care, and management of each cat, right down to the last details of the eventual adoption.

There was also the matter of medical supplies. Des had Bruce order vaccines and SNAP tests, used to diagnose feline immunodeficiency virus and feline leukemia virus, as well as latex gloves and temporary ID collars.

In truth, though, no number of meetings could have prepared the guys for the actuality of the all-day job of assessing and vaccinating the first bunch of cats. Their goal was fifty. The woman was expecting them, and everyone was on hand for this mission—G, Batso, Big Ant, Eric, Angel, Johnny O, Joe, and of course the cat guy, Des. The smell in the house was even more overpowering than it had been on their first visit several weeks before. Big Ant compared the experience of the smell in the house to having an ammonia-doused rag held over one's face. Everyone put on latex gloves, but the guys soon had to abandon any plans to wear the surgical masks they had brought along to filter out some of the smell: The woman recoiled when Big Ant walked in wearing one, taking offense at the implication that her house was unsanitary. Big Ant explained diplomatically that he was allergic to cats, but the Dr. Kildare look was a no-no from that point on.

The first step was catching some of the cats, which were understandably unsettled by this intrusion into their home. The men scoured the first floor, finding cats hunkered down behind the desks and stacks of old printers in a spare room. Lifting up the worn couch in the living room yielded a mother lode—there were about a dozen cats pressed up against the wooden frame, blinking in surprise that their hiding place had been breached. Even the recliner where the woman's elderly mother spent most of her time puffing on cigarettes was a condo of sorts for three cats, including a luminous-eyed gray who retreated still farther, until he was pressed up against the seat coils.

Rounding up the cats was easy at first: The calmest and friendliest let themselves be plucked off the tops of cabinets and windowsills. But as the day wore on, the remaining cats proved more elusive, and the guys soon had to strategize, herding some of the wilier ones into a small, empty spare bedroom where they could be grabbed quickly by the scruff and caught.

Some of the cats were young and easy to capture, like a gray youngster who was also a "Hemmie"—shorthand for Hemingway cat, because the famous author kept a colony of polydactyl (many-toed) cats at his home in Key West, Florida, where their descendants live even today. Others were older, wiser cats who made their displeasure at being caught abundantly known by hissing or trying daredevil escapes like bouncing off windows and kitchen appliances like furry Ping-Pong balls.

As the roundup began, the vet who had volunteered his services for the day set up his examination area on the counter between the kitchen and dining room. Dr. Alan Dubowy, a veterinarian from the Community Animal Hospital in Union Beach, New Jersey, had worked with Des on other cat rescues and was familiar with Des's method of documentation. Assisted by two vet techs from his practice, he gave each cat an exam, calling out his findings as Johnny O noted them on the intake sheet.

During the exam, the vet techs held each cat securely to prevent any attempt at escape, then drew blood for a SNAP test and placed a numbered identification collar that corresponded to the intake form around the cat's neck. From there, each cat was passed on to two more volunteer vet techs from the ASPCA, who administered the recommended vaccines and medications.

Unless it was pregnant, very underweight, or visibly ill, every cat was vaccinated for rabies as well as given a four-in-one vaccine to protect from panleukopenia (commonly known as feline distemper) and the three common causes of upper-respiratory infection: rhinotracheitis, chlamydia, and feline calisivirus. Each healthy cat also received a dose of Strongid, a worming medication, as well as a dose of Revolution, a treatment for parasites such as fleas, heartworm, ear mites, hookworm, and roundworm.

Finally, each cat was placed in a holding crate to keep it separated from the rest of the cats in the house. Rescue Ink would be back the next day to take the screened cats to be spayed and neutered.

As Dr. Dubowy was examining his tenth cat or so, he realized that the same diagnoses were cropping up again and again: Every cat had an ear-mite infestation and infection in both ears. And several of the cats had crumpled, wizened ears, the result of untreated hematomas. As the ear infections had been left untreated and progressed in severity, the cats constantly shook their heads at the discomfort, causing a blood blister, or hematoma, to form in the ear flap. Sometimes the hematoma grew large, resembling a big, fat sausage. Eventually the body reabsorbed the blood, but the ear cartilage shrank back only as much as the stretched skin would allow, creating what boxers call a cauliflower ear. It was painless but not very pretty.

There was, however, some good news: According to the SNAP tests, none of the cats tested so far were positive for feline immunodeficiency virus; closely related to the human virus, this can develop into feline AIDS, leaving the immunocompromised cat susceptible to opportunistic infections, though the disease is not transmissible to humans. They were also negative for feline leukemia, another incurable viral disease. Even though some cats were undernourished, some had upper respiratory infections, and all suffered raging ear infections and mite infestations, Dr. Dubowy pronounced the majority of the cats to be in generally good health.

Skittering around the house with the cats and the Rescue Ink guys trying to catch them were the local news media, who had been alerted by Rescue Ink in the hopes the press would help with adoptions. Enticed by the story, television crews and newspaper reporters huddled in the doorway, occasionally shooed back by G or Big Ant as the vet and techs went about their work. But as soon as the Rescue Ink guys became absorbed in their cat-catching, the reporters crept forward across the threshold, vying for shots of cats receiving vaccinations or having their blood drawn.

The goal for the day had been fifty cats, and Rescue Ink had accomplished almost half of the task when the woman who owned the house came up from the basement carrying basketsful of kittens. First she brought up a quintet of four-week-olds—including an adorable male tabby with front paws that resembled baseball mitts, thanks to his extra front "Hemmie" toes. A few minutes later she resurfaced with a batch of still-nursing kittens, a couple of weeks younger. And finally she brought up a litter of newborns who couldn't have been more than a few days old, their eyes still unopened.

By late afternoon, the media had gone. All the first-floor cats had been caught; the rest had fled to the basement, which the woman would not allow anyone to visit. The only one that remained was a huge white-and-black cat who was staying, one of several that the family wanted to keep. He must have realized his diplomatic immunity, as he had spent the entire day perched on a cat carrier in the middle of all the hubbub, looking alternately amused and bored, occasionally twitching his nose.

If animal-rescue hell existed, then Joe Panz was in it.

On this January evening, more than twenty-four hours after the big cat-house roundup, Joe was not only in the Center Moriches house, now with dozens fewer cats since the kittens had been whisked out the day before, but at its epicenter: the once off-limits basement. Acknowledging that all the cats were congregating there, the woman had finally agreed to let him downstairs.

Joe, Big Ant, Johnny O, and Bruce had come back in shifts to pick up the thirty adult cats that had been processed the day before with Dr. Dubowy to have them spayed and neutered. In fact, this was their second trip; they had picked up the first ten that morning. The back of the van was loaded with empty cat carriers borrowed from veterinarians and rescue groups from across the whole of Long Island.

But when they opened the door to the spare bedroom where the remainder of the screened cats were to have been sequestered, they found only ten; where were the other ten? Some of the cats had gotten loose, the woman explained. And some, she had decided, would not be leaving because she intended to keep them after the move.

The guys resisted the urge to roll their eyes; there was nothing they could do now, and there was no use arguing with her. But Des had arranged for a certain number of cats to be spayed and neutered that next morning, and the guys quickly decided to capture some more cats to make up the difference so the low-cost spay-neuter slots wouldn't be wasted.

By now, they knew exactly where to look for the hiding cats, including inside Old Faithful, the threadbare couch. But after about half an hour, they were still several cats short of the ten more they needed. That's when Joe decided to try the basement. When Joe descended the wooden steps, cats scattered in front of him like furry pool balls right after the break. Then they disappeared.

It had seemed impossible that the stench that permeated the house could be any worse, but it was far stronger down there. Joe took the skull bandana that he wore when riding his Harley and tied it cowboy style across his face and nose—not that it did much good. Like the rest of his clothing, the bandana's fabric just absorbed the house's pungent, ammonia-like odor, making it linger in his nostrils.

All around Joe were plenty of kitty-friendly hiding places—empty boxes or unzipped suitcases to hide in, a battered washing machine to duck behind, even a wall with a gaping hole in the plasterboard that made a convenient entry point for an excellent and hard-to-reach spot. Everything was covered in a layer of grime, the composition of which he didn't even want to contemplate. Clearly, this was where the cats lived, bred, and, obviously, urinated and defecated. It was like a room-size litter box.

"Any more?" someone yelled down to the basement. Joe contemplated the irony. Here was a house full of cats, yet all its whiskered residents had seemingly disappeared. As Joe looked up toward a hole in the ceiling, two moon eyes looked back at him, widening as he peered closer. The cat was big, it was mad, and it looked like it would launch like a missile if pushed too far. On a hunch, Joe laid his palm flat against the ceiling tile above his head and pushed gently. He felt a weight, then the sound of something scuffling away. Now he understood why the house's cats had disappeared as completely as Mr. Spock beaming up in the transporter. They were hiding— dozens upon dozens of them—in the basement ceiling.

"This," said Joe, repeating a pun he must have used twenty times that week, "is a cat-astrophe."

Rescue Ink tends to attract a media circus wherever it goes. So perhaps it is fitting that their home base is in a place whose name evokes the world's greatest showman, P. T. Barnum.

For decades, Barnum Island, better known to Long Islanders as Island Park, the adjacent island with which it shares a ZIP code and school district, was rumored to be associated with that famous circus impresario. Just across the bridge from the city of Long Beach, with its stuccoed mansions and grand boardwalk, Barnum Island is a humble little island of bungalows and a series of popular bars and nightclubs at the water's edge. Some residents note with pride that their one-mile-square patch of land is where P. T. Barnum used to winter his circus animals when the big top folded for the season.

The truth, however, is far less exotic. Barnum Island was indeed owned by a Barnum—the widow of clothier Peter Crosby Barnum—who purchased it in 1874, thwarting developers who envisioned a summer resort, so she could open an almshouse, or poorhouse. The island, which had previously been called Hog Island, a reference to the pigs that colonists had reared there, was subsequently renamed Barnum Island in her family's honor. Somewhere over the years, the two unrelated Barnums had been confused and made into one folkloric composite. In fact, the closest things to circus animals to get to Barnum Island were elephants brought over from Coney Island to haul logs across the marshes to help build the neighboring Long Beach boardwalk in the early 1900s. Some of the laborers, but none of the pachyderms, stayed on Barnum Island. The island as it exists today came from modest people and modest beginnings.

In the fall of 2008, Rescue Ink finally saw its dream of establishing a home base realized. It relocated its operations from the various diners and Dunkin' Donuts the guys used to frequent to a small boatyard owned by George Voutsinas, ubiquitously known as Junior, on Barnum Island, right on the water's edge. Junior had reached out to the guys when he saw them on *The Ellen DeGeneres Show* in June 2008. A longtime supporter of local rescue groups and an avid rescuer himself, he threw a benefit at his catering hall for the group that October, and then let them use the unoccupied Barnum Island property as their headquarters. Surrounded by marinas and construction yards, it was a scrappy locale for an equally scrappy bunch.

"When we moved in here, the guy who owns the boatyard next door came over and told me about each and every body and body part that ever washed up here," says Bruce with a chuckle.

But the small house on the three-quarter-acre property was no laughing matter. Built in the 1970s, it had never seen an update, from its wood-paneled walls to its chocolate-brown stove. As the newest member at the time, Eric was recruited to cover the interior with a fresh coat of paint, an assignment he took on in his usual taciturn way.

For decor, there were black leather chairs salvaged from a defunct law firm someone had a connection to. The coffee table held an automatic card shuffler and a bunch of hot-rod magazines with names like *Ol' Skool Rodz* and *Car Kulture DeLuxe*. Inside their pages were highboy roadsters and tricked-up Model A coupes with decidedly un-airbrushed women in hot pants posing in front of them or draped across their fenders. The front bedroom was soon converted into an office, with two donated computers. A printer was needed, but would have to wait. For an added air of mystery, the floor had a trapdoor.

The Rescue Ink members had thought their out-of-the-way clubhouse would be a quiet place to meet, go over cases, and, in the summer, grill burgers and throw back a few beers in the backyard overlooking the placid canal. Instead, in the aftermath of the cat rescue, the clubhouse turned into a cat house—and not the kind, ahem, that a single guy might like to visit.

After the cats returned from their surgeries, they needed a place to convalesce. So the guys turned one of the spare bedrooms into a cat room, complete with litter boxes, food and water bowls, open crates, and Rubbermaid containers made into cat shelters for the displaced cats to hide.

With long showers and a total change of clothes, the guys had managed to rid themselves of the memory of the smell of the house in Center Moriches. But now it suffused the one-story clubhouse, carried in on the cats themselves. Even if the guys could bathe the frightened, overwhelmed cats—where would they begin? with Kevlar gloves?—it was unlikely that it would do much. The odor seemed embedded in the cats' fur, like an essence.

In the aftermath of the previous day's great escape at the Center Moriches house, it was clear that Rescue Ink needed a new approach. Vetting the cats at the house and then leaving them there while they awaited transport to the vet's for surgery would not work, as there was no guarantee that the woman wouldn't set them free for whatever reason. And the cats would probably be less stressed convalescing in a familiar environment. So they had left a bunch of carriers and some instructions for the woman. The day before Rescue Ink was scheduled to come, she would put the spay-neuter candidates into the carriers and have them ready. After the surgeries, Rescue Ink would return to the house with the altered and newly vaccinated cats and let them back into the population for the time being.

It wasn't a perfect solution, but at least it would stanch the population growth at the house. And Rescue Ink needed time to adopt out the dozens of cats it already had who were making themselves at home in the spare bedroom at the clubhouse. (One heavily pregnant female had already had kittens, and she was nursing them in the shower stall in one of the two bathrooms.)

Like many suburban areas, Long Island is woefully lacking in feral-cat advocacy groups. The few that exist are overwhelmed with requests for help with trap, neuter, and return (TNR) efforts, and often loan out traps to residents who want to take on some responsibility themselves for stopping the population explosion.

The cat group near Rescue Ink had raised enough funds to buy a construction-style trailer that was stationed in a parking lot behind city hall in nearby Long Beach. The group had offered to spay and neuter some of the Center Moriches cats at a reduced fee, and its president, Nancy Vogt, had visited them at the clubhouse to make sure the cats were recovering well. She volunteered to come over several times a day to monitor, feed, and clean up after the residents of the cat room. She also explained the miraculous odor-reducing properties of Febreze to the guys.

Getting a bunch of dog-centric manly men up to speed on the specifics of cat caretaking was a challenge, and there was a learning curve, to say the least. After the first night the cats spent in the spare room at the clubhouse, it became readily apparent that not all were using the litter boxes that Nancy had set up. The carpet looked like a Jackson Pollock painting restricted to an earth-tone palette, so Joe made a midnight trip to Home Depot and, with cursing that could be heard by G and Batso in Connecticut, ripped up the foul carpeting and replaced it with linoleum.

"We have the determination and we love the animals and we're gonna do whatever it takes to get the job done," Joe said. "And, quite frankly, nobody else is stepping up to the plate. So we're all together on this, we're gonna come through and it's gonna be fun."

Absently, he scratched the cat bite on his arm.

As the Rescue Ink guys who lived closest to the cat house—Big Ant, Johnny O, Joe, and Bruce—planned another run to the house to get another batch of cats to be spayed and neutered, Des worked the phones to line up more low-cost surgeries as well as talk to rescue groups that could take some of the friendlier cats. While none of the cats were truly feral, since they had grown up in close contact with humans, most were frightened and skittish and needed time to convince themselves that these new people weren't as scary as they thought.

"Cats can be a very affectionate type of animal, but it's an affection that you have to win. Pretty much the way you earn the affection of your friends and your lovers and your wives and your girlfriends and anybody else that's meaningful in your life," says Des philosophically. "There's a period of time where you don't know your positioning, and you work for it. And then all of a sudden, the relationship is established and it's yours, it belongs to you, it's something tangible. You can feel it, you can touch it."

Several days a week, Des mustered up the time and energy to do his six-hour round-trip commute to the clubhouse. On one of those visits, another group of cats had come back from being spayed and neutered. One thin little cat had been placed close to the heat register to keep her warm, but when Des looked through the carrier's wire door, he didn't see any movement. Just a motionless figure wrapped tightly inside a blanket. His concern ballooning, Des quickly undid the screws that held the carrier's top and bottom halves together, and uncovered the little calico. She was motionless and cold to the touch. Nancy, who was at the clubhouse doing her daily check of the cats, immediately heated up a rice sock in the microwave, wrapped it in a towel, and placed it next to the chilled cat. Des checked the cat's gums. They looked paler than he would have liked. Her body temperature was not rising. His worst fear was that she might be hemorrhaging internally, or going into shock.

Bundling her back up in the carrier, he headed to the nearby vet's office, where Spike had had his neuter surgery a few weeks before. Dr. Ratner whisked the cat to the back room, and Des paced in the waiting room for what seemed to him like an eternity.

Finally, Dr. Ratner called him into the exam room. The cat was in the back, she explained, warming up under some heat lamps. Her tongue was still pink, signaling that internal bleeding was not likely. She was just very chilled; when her temperature was taken, the mercury had not budged from the bottom of the thermometer. A few hours under the heat lamp should do the trick, Dr. Ratner assured Des.

He breathed a sigh of relief. Though Rescue Ink had taken dozens of cats out of that house, the well-being of each and every one weighed on him equally. And as he remembered the cold feeling of the calico cat under his hand, that weight of responsibility pressed in on him from all sides.

"This Kitty Adoption Event is ON and it's meeeow," read the posting on craigslist. Its slightly loopy humor hinted strongly at Des's authorship.

Rescue Ink's first cat adoption event was scheduled for a chilly Sunday in January. The announcement gave the location—on the sidewalk on New York's Upper West Side—as well as all the details about the cats: They had been vaccinated, wormed, spayed or neutered, and tested for feline leukemia virus (FeLV) and feline immune deficiency virus (FIV). Included in the adoption was a cat-adoption coupon book worth $100 and redeemable at a local Petco store and "unlimited, life-time, 24/7 post-adoption technical support: You have a PROBLEM?" the posting asked rhetorically. "We take cats back no matter the reason or years passed. We're more fun," it concluded, "and double the snuggles."

Big Ant, Johnny O, and Joe had no idea what to expect when the Rescue Ink van pulled up on Broadway at the corner of Eighty-second Street. They had brought seven cats from the clubhouse, including the little gray Hemmie and a female of the same color and age who they guessed might be his sister. Angel and G were already there, milling in front of Des's adoption display.

Long before he became a member of Rescue Ink, Des had been adopting out cats on this stretch of sidewalk. "I went out to the street with the cats and it took me three months before anybody even talked to me, for people to even say hello. Then it took another three months before I actually had one adoption," Des remembers. "Here's a guy on the street with a bunch of cats, I mean, who is this crazy guy, right? But now if I'm not there it seems odd and the locals miss me, as they tell me when I come back."

The key to real estate is location, location, location, and on this well-trafficked corner Des had found a perfect reservoir of potential homes. "The people on the Upper West Side are fabulous. For the most part, they're intelligent. You don't have to twist people's arms to talk them into a vaccine," he explains. "I can find homes for the cats that are suitable, and stable, and, in some cases, plush, you know. A big plasma screen for the cat to watch TV, I mean, how sweet is that? It's a better life than I'm having."

Des's sidewalk setup was a work of elaborate engineering, a veritable kitty biosphere. On top of a sturdy wooden table he had secured three medium-size wire dog crates with three more stacked on top of those. Heavy-ply plastic sheeting covered the entire bank of cages and was secured with large clamps. At the curb, a heavy-duty generator buzzed, pumping heat into the six compartments. Des had a backup at the ready just in case it stopped operating. Inside each crate was a snuggly bed and either a cat hammock or a wooden platform for its resident to climb and explore. And in the crate at the top of this Taj Mahal of makeshift adoption centers was an outdoor thermometer, decorated with a beach scene. Its black arm pointed to a balmy 85 degrees. Outside the crates, it was barely above freezing.

With G's and Angel's help, Big Ant, Joe, and Johnny unloaded the carriers from the van and brought them over to Des on the sidewalk. Carefully, he took out each cat and placed it in one of the crates. The two gray siblings took up residence in one of the bottom crates, where they crept into a hammock, nuzzled each other, and fell fast asleep.

"They all know him on this corner," said an impressed Big Ant, as various women in expensive coats and Prada bags stopped to chat and catch up with Des. "It must be nice in summertime," he added, thinking how comfy the cats must be inside their oasis. If their body language was any indication, the cats were enjoying their balmy quarters. One of the calicos watched the passersby with great interest, occasionally blinking its eyes in contentment.

"Take a cat or he's getting it," Big Ant joked, grabbing Des by the neck.

But Des had a more professional adoption strategy. Anyone who was interested in a cat filled out an adoption form and paid a $5 application fee, which was a simple way for him to weed out those who weren't really serious about adopting. The strategy worked. From 1:00 to 5:00 P.M., dozens of people stopped to admire the cats and ask about how they had been rescued. And by the end of the day, there were five applicants. Des scanned the paperwork. Two were iffy—one had very vague references, and the other didn't seem stable enough. But the remaining three were quite promising, especially the very last one.

Crissa had read about the adoption event online, and had come all the way from Fort Lee, New Jersey, with her son, seven-year-old Eli, to see the cats. The family had just lost their beloved cat Puck after thirteen years. Eli had never known life without his furry friend, and was devastated. Eli zeroed in on the two gray kittens, looking longingly through the plastic sheeting. He wanted them both.

Des read through the adoption application. It was impeccable. Crissa was an experienced cat owner. She had a vet who, when Des called, vouched for her, describing how Crissa had spared no expense in caring for her sick Puck until the bitter end. And she had made the trip all the way across the river. She was serious. Des usually doesn't make an on-the-spot adoption from the sidewalk. But this was a special case. These kittens needed to be in a home sooner rather than later so they could continue their socialization. And Eli needed some feline companionship to fill the void that Puck had left.

Eli couldn't contain his excitement as Des gently extracted the two kittens from the cage and put them in the carrier. "Mommy, Mommy!" he exclaimed. "Can I name them? You got to name Puck!"

Crissa had her car waiting a few feet away, and before the kittens could get a chill, Eli clambered in, and she set the carrier on his lap. The kittens were headed for the Lincoln Tunnel, beyond which a whole new life would open up.

Two down, 178 to go.

11

Mary and Bruce

Hers and His

The adoption van was parked in a shopping-center parking lot in Oceanside, just a few miles from Rescue Ink's clubhouse. Milling in front of the vehicle were a bunch of dogs wearing bright orange vests that read "Adopt Me." At the end of their leashes were a handful of Rescue Ink members who had been invited there by a local rescue group, Bobbi and the Strays, to help find homes for these down-on-their-luck pups.

A woman walked up, but she went right past Eric, who was petting and holding the leash of a young Rottie mix named Brody. She passed up Big Ant and a handsome pit bull named Marshall, and Junior with Marcos, a chocolate-colored pit-Lab mix who was scarred up from being used as a bait dog. Instead, she zeroed in on a doggie baby carriage pushed by Mary Fayet, Rescue Ink's operations coordinator.

Persuaded by the woman's persistent coos, Mary unzipped the carriage's mesh cover and extracted a little dog in a blue-and-yellow sweater named George.

"He was found at the bottom of a Dumpster in the Bronx,"

Mary explained, setting the little Maltipoo—that's shorthand for the so-called designer breed cross between a Maltese and a poodle—on the asphalt. "Someone hit him with a blunt object," she continued, as the bundle of white fur, whom Mary estimated to be four or five years old, took a few hesitant steps forward.

When Mary first took George in as a foster from another rescue group two weeks before, he had the strange habit of turning himself in circles nonstop, likely the result of being crated almost constantly. More confirmation of his previous imprisonment in impossibly tight quarters showed in how he went to the bathroom: He would find a corner in a room and back himself up to it so that his hind legs were halfway up the wall. And George's tail had a perpetual curve to the right, as if he'd never had room to straighten it out.

The vet initially thought George might have had a stroke or brain damage and didn't think he would survive the anesthesia for his neutering. "But he surprises me every day," says Mary, who let George have the run of the house with her pack of pint-size dogs as soon as he arrived at her house. "He never had toys before, and he's acting like a puppy probably for the first time, like he reverted back."

Mary, who had her long black hair pulled into a ponytail and threaded through the back of her Rescue Ink cap, hadn't brought George to this adoption event to find him a home. In fact, she already had several prospective applicants waiting for the opportunity to adopt him. But before he was ready for a loving forever home, he needed to be exposed to the wide world and his reactions observed.

"I thought it would take me two months to turn this dog around," said Mary, watching as George greeted the woman who had asked to see him. But after just two short weeks, it looked like he had turned a corner.

Mary, forty-eight, is the closest thing Rescue Ink has to a den mother. She joined the group in March 2008 after Angel referred her to the guys. It was becoming increasingly clear that the group needed someone with experience to handle phone calls and e-mails while the guys were busy in the field. Her day starts at 7:00 A.M. and ends at 10:00 or 11:00 at night, when she finally shuts off her computer. Wearing her ever-present headset, Mary takes complaints and tips and forwards them on to the group for discussion and, if investigation proves them to be legitimate, action. She helps locate resources, from trainers to veterinarians to foster homes. And she counsels clueless and confused owners from Brooklyn to Brisbane who find Rescue Ink's toll-free number and e-mail address on the Internet, though she was hard-pressed to offer much help to the South African woman who wanted to bail out sixteen lions that she read were to be euthanized because their keepers could no long afford to feed them.

Sometimes geography is not an issue, and she can resolve things right on the phone. When a soldier who was being deployed to Iraq called about giving up his dog, she pointed him to groups that specifically find foster homes for the pets of military personnel during their tours of duty. When a woman from Las Vegas e-mailed to say she needed to find a new home for her Weimaraner, who had come to be out of control after it had been left out in the yard for most of its puppyhood while she recovered from a broken leg, Mary helped find her a trainer to teach the beautiful gray dog some manners.

"It's not brain science," Mary sighs. "A lot of times people don't need a bunch of burly tattooed men to set up a trap or knock on a door. They just need encouragement."

Dogs like George frequently arrive in Mary's care with a sad story, but often no name. And it just so happens with those anonymous male rescues that Mary will find inspiration and a namesake among the Rescue Ink guys. Sometimes it's whoever pops into her head, as was the case with George. Other times, it's the name of whichever guy has most recently annoyed her for any number of reasons. That's why she christened a pit bull–boxer mix Bruce, a name that stuck even after he went to his new home. And in a real fit of exasperation at Joe, she named a six-year-old Maltese Joey. To add insult to injury, the dog was a hermaphrodite, and needed to be spayed as well as neutered to remove both sets of sex organs. "That's because people are always telling me to go screw myself," Joe said with a shrug.

As for dealing with Rescue Ink's very guy-centric approach, "I am definitely surrounded by a lot of testosterone," admits Mary, who knows a little bit about male culture: She has been married for twenty-nine years to a now-retired navy man. Raising three sons, who are now all in their twenties, "definitely prepared me for Rescue Ink," she continues. And she knows from tough: Mary worked at a treatment center for children with behavioral problems who had also committed sexual offenses.

"The guys are very street, and sometimes you gotta be as nasty as they are," she says matter-of-factly about her Rescue Ink colleagues. When she sent an animated e-mail and got a response that read, "You can take the exclamation points and shove them up your ass," she gave back as good as she got. And then all was forgotten.

If there is a silver lining to such raw interactions, it's that wounds are quickly healed and forgotten. "Boys are different," Mary explains. "When you tell a girl she can't sleep over Susie's on Friday night, she's crying and whining for days. When you tell a boy he can't go over Frankie's house, he's gonna stomp off to his room, mutter under his breath, slam the door, and then come out for dinner like nothing happened. That's how it is with the guys—they blow up, and then it's all right."

At the adoption event, Big Ant winced as he looked over and saw George's powder-puff physique. Mary's penchant for Malteses and other toy dogs doesn't always resonate with the group's affection for more masculine breeds like Rotties and pits. Neither does her fondness for dressing them up in everything from coveralls to pajamas.

No matter. The sun had disappeared behind midwinter clouds, and George was getting chilled, even with his sporty sweater. Mary let the woman say her good-byes, then packed George back in the baby carriage. As maiden voyages go, George's had been a good one.

Several weeks after the adoption event, Mary was back in her usual spot: her home office in the Bronx. Though she is more than welcome to operate out of the Rescue Ink clubhouse, her spare-bedroom office, with its L-shaped glass desk, is really her home base in every sense of the word. And while she can appreciate the *Reservoir Dogs* posters and water views of the clubhouse's dated, wood-paneled main room, Mary would prefer to be surrounded by her ever-shifting pack of at least nine dogs, who keep her company as she sips her Dunkin' Donuts coffee and starts her workday.

At the top of the heap is alpha dog Sarge, an aptly named

miniature pinscher–Chihuahua mix who struts around like he owns the place, which in truth he pretty much does. His other buddies are, like him, all rescues Mary has adopted. Among the nine is Simon, the four-year-old poodle who is terrified of umbrellas and leashes and is so neurotic he lives mostly under Mary's bed. And Madison, a diva of a Maltese, feels it is her role in life to communicate to Simon her low opinion of him. Parker is a one-year-old Maltese with a charming pretty-boy insouciance. Tyson the orange tabby cat, a former burn victim, at twenty-two pounds is the largest animal in the house.

For the last fifteen years, ever since she fostered her first Maltese, an elderly dog named Dewey Louie whose death shattered her heart, Mary has devoted herself to rescuing toy dogs that are senior citizens. Despite her husband's insistence that she can't add any more to the household, sometimes she simply cannot bear to part with one. "So I've found a new term: forever foster," Mary says. Falling into this category are two more Malteses: ancient, toothless Luigi, and Diamond, who has a low-functioning liver and is not expected to live for more than a few more months.

Rotating through this permanent pack are the real fosters, who are just passing through on their way to their forever homes. George the Dumpster-tossed Maltese is no longer residing at Mary's. The day after the adoption event in February, he found a new home with Miriam Dolin and Christopher Young in Manhattan. Broadway lovers, they promptly named him Oliver Twist—a fitting name for an orphan like him. "He is the light of our lives," says Miriam. "He has his own groomer, trainer, and dog walker, and a brand-new wardrobe. We curl up together every night." Oliver has an adoptive cousin, another Maltipoo named Norman, who has taken it upon himself to continue Oliver's education on how to play with toys.

With George/Oliver gone, Mary had already taken in a new batch of fosters: siblings Bam Bam and Pebbles, who look like Chihuahua-papillon mixes, and Chewie, a one-and-a-half-year-old Tibetan spaniel that Angel called to tell Mary about after the dog was left at a Bronx police precinct. Chewie was hyperactive and bark-happy, and Mary was not pleased. Had Chewie not arrived with a name of his own, Mary would have reached for "Angel" in a heartbeat.

Mary put on her headset and settled behind the desk, where a couple dozen e-mails were already awaiting her: A man on Long Island has a Newfoundland who got loose and bit several people, and is scheduled to be euthanized. A woman in Manhattan explains that her dog has a weeping tumor on her belly, but she has no money to go to the vet. And someone in Missouri alerts Mary to a case of horse neglect.

One by one, with a little Googling in between, Mary answered all the e-mails, her responses a blend of sympathy and pragmatism. She referred the Newfie owner to an attorney known for defending animal cases (though she noted that no rescue group would willingly take on a known biter). She pointed the owner of the sick dog to a New York City program called Safety Net, which assists owners down on resources with medical care for their pets. And she contacted a senior cruelty investigator from an equine rescue society about the Missouri case.

"Part of my job is finding out what the problem is, which is not necessarily what they're telling you," Mary observes. "A caller might say they have to get rid of the dog because it has allergies, then you find out it has aggression issues. Sometimes they're screaming, and I tell them, Go take a walk and call me back when you've calmed down."

The biggest problem, she thinks, is how disconnected we are as a society. Many people are strangers to their own neighbors, and are quick to assign blame rather than extend a hand and see if they can help on their own. "We are all so willing to rat and tattle anonymously, because we can hide behind computers and cell phones. Where is the compassion that our grandparents had?" asks Mary, remembering the eighty-year-old woman who wanted Rescue Ink to give her neighbor a beat-down because the family dog was matted and ill groomed. Mary investigated, and found that the family was facing foreclosure. "They didn't have the money for a groomer—it might have meant gas in the tank or milk for the kids," she says. "Does that mean they are bad people? Not one person in the neighborhood reached out. You have energy to call me up, but have you talked to your neighbor?" Rescue Ink arranged to have the dog groomed— something the neighbors could have easily done themselves if they had only exercised the very compassion and care that they accused the dog's owners of lacking.

Luigi whined, so Mary scooped the three-pound Maltese up from the floor and placed him on the glass desk. It was too high for him to jump off, so he settled down among her papers in resignation. E-mails dispatched, Mary moved on to her project for the day, a novel one for her: finding a home for a five-foot-long alligator named Mason.

Mason was rescued from a college dorm where his mouth had been duct-taped shut. When his undergraduate captors did unmuzzle him, it was only to feed him or use him for enter-tainment; their idea of the latter was to let him chomp on PVC pipe, which resulted in a mouthful of broken teeth. For the last two years, Mason had been with Second Chance Animal Rescue in Farmingville, in eastern Long Island, which is run by federally licensed wildlife rehabilitators. But Mason's enclosure was growing a little snug, and Rescue Ink had offered to help Second Chance secure him a new home with more elbow room. Second Chance hoped Mason would be placed at a facility in the metropolitan area that would continue to use him for education and outreach about crocodilian species. Mary dialed up a New Jersey facility called Popcorn Park, made a pitch for Mason, and was promised a callback once the head zookeeper was consulted.

Then the phone rang again, and it was back to more mundane fare: A cocker spaniel puppy had just been dumped at a local grooming shop—could Mary take him?

With a sigh, Mary set Luigi back on the ground and hunted for her car keys. It looked like her little pack was going to expand just a tiny bit more.

If Rescue Ink has a runt of the litter, it's Bruce Feinberg, the group's media liaison and all-purpose fire-douser. He'll not only admit to the description, it's the one he cheerfully offers by way of explaining how his slim, self-effacing self fits in among a group of hulking guys whose upper arms are bigger than his thighs.

"Certainly, I am the 'What's wrong with this picture?'" he admits. "When someone asks, 'What's his role?' the guys say, 'He's the one who reads and writes.'"

Like Mary, Bruce, who is fifty-five, is an indispensable behind-the-scenes necessity for Rescue Ink. He's not always out on the street with the guys knocking on doors, but he's there for the phone calls lamenting "I lost my keys" and "I'm out of gas." "I'm the human GPS," he says. "I've navigated guys when they were driving down two-lane country roads headed straight for Lake Huron."

Bruce fields most of his calls at home, a typical bachelor pad that is just a mile or so from the clubhouse. The two-bedroom apartment comprises the top level of a two-family house and is decorated in a style he calls "Early Chaos." It's a literal home office, with a baby grand in the living room, audio gear everywhere, and a profusion of everything Rescue Ink throughout, from logoed T-shirts to temporary tattoos to itineraries from past rescues.

Navigating the uneven steps in late February, Bruce unlocked the door to the clubhouse. Nancy and her crew of volunteers had brought in industrial-strength air fresheners, but the cat smell persisted. Ducking into the spare bedroom, Bruce checked on the twenty or so cats that still resided there while they waited for the adoption event, and noted with satisfaction, and not a little relief, that the cat ladies had cleaned the litter boxes. On the table was a list from Nancy of the supplies he needed to pick up on his next Costco run: paper towels, kitty litter, and antiseptic wipes.

Being a pop-culture-riffing intellectual amid a bunch of burly bikers and street toughs is hardly out of character for Bruce, whose entire life has pretty much been a series of incongruities. He grew up in relatively rural, overwhelmingly Catholic Patchogue, Long Island, where his family had farmed for generations and later run a duck-dressing plant. "I'm a feral Jew," he says blithely. "Ever smell a duck farm in summer? It'll cauterize your nose."

Bruce went on to college at Jesuit-run Georgetown University, where his English-lit professor was slightly perplexed at his blank-faced admission that he hadn't read the book. He didn't mean the assigned text, *Murder in the Cathedral*, Bruce eventually explained; he meant the New Testament.

At Georgetown, Bruce attended the Edmund A. Walsh School of Foreign Service, an academic incubator for aspiring diplomats. But turned off by the rootlessness of the military and diplomatic brats he met in the program, Bruce followed his fascination for music and the performing arts, and fell into a job as the business manager of a stage-lighting company. Soon enough he was on the road as a "lightie," hanging out with backstage crews that shared more than a passing resemblance to Rescue Ink—big guys who lived hard and laughed loud.

"You know what I like about you, Feinberg?" Bruce remembers a roadie grunting to him one day. "You're ignorant. I don't have to unlearn you any bad habits."

Later, Bruce crisscrossed the country as a drum and guitar roadie. On Vegas casino gigs, he worked two hours a day and gambled for six. He was on Mount Saint Helens the day the volcano blew, when it turned pitch-black at three in the afternoon and the birds sang their evening songs. He lived on a tour bus, subsisting on beef jerky and the refrigerated section of whatever Piggly Wiggly was nearby.

In 1981, Bruce came back to his native Long Island, cut his hair, got married, and landed a job as an assistant director of New York City mayor Ed Koch's Office of Film, Theater and Broadcasting. By the mid-1990s, he was appointed by then-governor Mario Cuomo as the director of the Governor's Film Office. Its headquarters were down at the Chelsea Piers in Manhattan, in the same swath of vaguely derelict waterfront that served as the set for *Law & Order*. The back door of Bruce's office led into the show's interrogation room stage set.

Throughout his zigzagging career path, Bruce has always been drawn to oversize personalities and interesting subcultures. "The funny thing is, I was always backstage or an emcee," he shrugs. "I never desired the spotlight."

Bruce was introduced to Rescue Ink by Robert in December 2007, and his involvement "just grew and grew," Bruce remembers. "I've always been an animal lover, but I didn't know anything about the world of animal rescue." A consummate wordsmith, Bruce started as the guy behind the desk who wrote press releases and scripted copy for the Web site. But he understood the pack dynamic of Rescue Ink, and he knew that on some level he would have to prove his mettle.

He met almost all the guys at his first Rescue Ink event. It was an adoptathon at North Shore Animal League in Port Washington. Being a pretty good shot with a camera, Bruce brought his. "When Ant asked me to take some shots of the guys doing their thing, in my best impression of a tough guy, I said, 'I didn't come here to take fucking pictures.'" After that hackle-raising response, "the pack started to accept me a little more," Bruce says. "Now I wasn't just the press liaison. They found I could be useful in my own right." But make no mistake—he still gets grief for wearing a mini-backpack, or, as the guys have termed it in their politically incorrect way, "the fag bag."

Bruce looked out the window of the clubhouse and calculated the remaining days until spring. Regardless of where he's lived, Bruce has always had a great garden, with fat, well-tended vegetables. Though it was only mid-February, he was already thinking about May, when the danger of frost would be past and he could plant his garden on the clubhouse grounds. Given the proximity to salt water, he'd need to build some raised beds, of course, and lug in some topsoil. And plenty of manure. There was an easy joke there, he knew.

Bruce acknowledges that he is sometimes taken aback by the fanaticism of some hard-core, longtime rescuers. "I'm a person who says there can be such a thing as an outside dog, as long as there's adequate food and shelter," he remarks. "A lot of it is cultural. Some people think, 'That's an animal, it lives outside the house.' We have to accept that we aren't going to change that, but we can communicate the message that the animal has to be taken care of even if it's not in the house."

Some cases Bruce finds downright frustrating, like the cat rescuer who called Rescue Ink because one of her cats disappeared. She lived in a relatively posh neighborhood, and had created an elaborate screened outdoor living space for her many cats. Wind chimes rang out every time the ocean breeze stirred, and the cats had running fountains and complex tunnel systems that led to different patios and outdoor vantage points. The problem was, she sometimes let the cats roam outside, a big no-no among most cat caretakers.

"She told us, 'People are running over my cats on purpose,' and she made up flyers and had us deliver them within a three-block radius, asking anyone who had information on the abusers to contact Rescue Ink," Bruce remembers. "We told her, people aren't trying to run down these cats—they're darting out into the road! If you love these cats, don't let them run loose." But she wouldn't acknowledge that she might be the source of her own problem.

Admittedly, Bruce isn't a diehard "dog person" or "cat person," but there might be an advantage to that: He can see the problems from a fresh perspective, alternative thinker that he is. "For example, why can't there be some kind of birth control for feral cats?" he asks rhetorically. "I look at the hundreds of thousands of hours that people put into trap, neuter, and return and it's like trying to bail out the ocean with a teacup. What if there was some other way to have population control and attrition?"

Bruce doesn't have a dog or cat at the moment; his apartment lease just doesn't permit it. But there are plenty of animals in his Rescue Ink orbit whose affection he appreciates and reciprocates. There is an all-black cat with eyes the color of faded emeralds who greets him effusively whenever he visits the clubhouse. And he is inordinately fond of Mary's Luigi, as doddering and fragile as the dog is. There is something incredibly appealing about animals like Luigi, who know who they are, limitations and all, and still demand to be recognized and respected.

Bruce tapped some food into the clubhouse fish tank, and its residents swarmed to the top. He noted with satisfaction that the two platys he bought the other day had been accepted by the tank's established school of fish and were swimming along placidly. Lucky fish.

Rescue Ink wants to be more than just muscle: If the guys can educate young people, and stop even one from becoming an abuser, that's one less door for them to knock on down the road.

Rescue Ink's Eyes & Ears campaign grew out of that desire, and Bruce, with the guys' input, has structured the school-based program and refined its message. Beyond just communicating that loving and rescuing animals is cool, Rescue Ink asks each schoolchild to commit to reporting abuse whenever he or she sees it.

"We're empowering them, deputizing them in a sense," Bruce explains. "They're the new generation, and we need them to help protect the animals from abuse and neglect."

On a Friday in January 2009, the Rescue Ink guys arrived for an assembly at the Park Avenue School in North Merrick. The grade school's fifth- and sixth-graders filed into the auditorium, trying hard not to stare at Batso's tattoo-covered head. Amused, Batso quacked at them with Donald Duck–like gusto, and they quickly regained their manners. "I wash them off at night," he teased one girl who had stopped with genuine admiration to get a better look at his body art.

The guys took turns introducing themselves: Joe, Big Ant, Johnny O, Des, Angel, Batso, and G. These kids were from relatively privileged homes, and that showed in everything from the confident, probing way in which they asked questions to the laundry list of purebred dog breeds they owned, from soft-coated wheaten terriers to Yorkies.

When it was his turn to speak, Big Ant drove home the message of adopting before buying. "The shelters are full of animals, especially now, when people are having a hard time keeping jobs and making money," he said. "Tell your parents to go to the shelter instead of stopping at the pet store. There are a lot of animals waiting for your love."

As the guys talked and fielded questions, Bruce watched carefully, making the occasional note about subjects that seemed to strike a particularly strong chord with the kids. When the time came, he went over to the laptop he had set up and pushed a button. The screen in front of the auditorium stage filled with the short film that Bruce conceived and produced on the theme "What rescue means to me," which tied for first place for Best Dogumentary at North Shore Animal League's 2008 DogCatemy Awards. When it was over, the words *Abusers are losers* appeared on the screen.

Every good tour manager knows that you gotta wow them with the finale, and Bruce had long ago perfected a dramatic capper to the Eyes & Ears program. "I'm going to introduce you to a member of Rescue Ink who was a New York City police detective, who has now dedicated his life to protecting animals," Joe began. "He's the guy who investigates the cases that are reported to us, so that we can go and make sure that any abuse or neglect is stopped, and that all the animals are taken care of."

Angel stepped forward and asked the children to stand. "Right hand up," he said in a commanding voice, and the students obligingly raised their hands. "Left foot in," he continued.

The children looked around at each other in mild confusion.

"Do the hokeypokey . . . no, that's not right," Angel said, breaking into a grin, and the room erupted in laughter.

Bruce had already printed up Junior Pet Investigator certificates and distributed them to the teachers, who would hand them out to the children when they returned to class. The official-looking pieces of paper reiterated the pledge that Angel had read to them: "I pledge to use my eyes and ears to help protect animals from abuse and neglect. If I see or hear of animals being mistreated or in need of help, I will report it at once to a grown-up: a parent, a teacher, or a police officer."

"Angel nailed it," said Bruce with satisfaction amid the happy buzz in the room. With a mixture of decorum and humor, Angel had communicated the importance of standing up and being counted on for the animals. It was a home run.

After the program, the children milled around, eager to talk about their own animals and how they might continue to help Rescue Ink, perhaps by making cat shelters as a class project.

"They are so real," Bruce says with genuine affection of the guys whose testosterone-fueled venting sometimes leads him to hold the phone a foot away from his ear. "Each of them is unique in his own way. None of them has the background of any other. It hasn't been the easiest of bunches to assimilate with, but I have.

"It's the high-school lunchroom, but we'll order any fucking thing we want" from the cafeteria counter, says Bruce affectionately of the Rescue Ink dynamic. And he is definitely at the cool table.

12

Angel

The Pet Detective

Maria was not an unattractive woman, to put it bluntly.
When she answered the door, the representatives of Rescue Ink assembled on her Brooklyn doorstep on this summer day in 2008 suddenly stopped complaining about wild goose chases. With this kind of scenery, her tube top, tight jeans, and a tattoo on the small of her back, who cared if this was the right address for an accused dognapper?

Well, Angel Nieves did. As he talked to the woman, "my brain was burning," he remembers, and not for the same reason as his colleagues'. They were smitten—he was suspicious.

"Everybody was saying, 'He's just rapping to her,'" in the hopes of scoring a date, Angel says. But the more he talked to the woman, whose real name is not Maria, the more convinced he became that he had found the person who was refusing to return a long-lost poodle back to its rightful owner. Maria cooed to Angel, explaining that she didn't know about any dog. This all must be a big misunderstanding. Anyway, she was on her way to a party. "All right, hon, take care," she said cheerfully to Angel as she concluded their conversation, hopped into her car, and drove off.

"That's her—she's got the dog," Angel said, turning to his still starry-eyed colleagues. He didn't have proof yet. But his instincts told him all he needed to know.

Forty-seven-year-old Angel, a retired New York City police detective and Rescue Ink's resident investigator, spends his spare time at the desk of his second-floor home office, scouring the Internet and running down leads. Most of the Rescue Ink guys aren't big on paperwork, but Angel is the one guy with the files, a huge accordion folder filled with leads and addresses and cell phone numbers. In the habit of investigating murders and drug deals from his time on the force, Angel is methodical, building each case piece by piece, lead by lead, phone call by phone call.

"I used to save people from animals," reads one of the banners on his MySpace page, a reference to the lowlifes he once locked up as a city cop. "Now I save animals from people."

Angel has the clipped, no-nonsense cadence of a career cop. Not much surprises him. At the 2008 Broadway Barks, a fundraiser by the Manhattan theater community for animal rescue, right in front of *Spamalot*, a canine spectator launched himself at Angel, nailing him in the chin. Angel didn't flinch, just stepped back. He doesn't blame the dog, but rather the clueless owner, who should have known better than to bring an undersocialized, overwhelmed rescue dog to a street fair with thousands of people and dogs. Angel grew a goatee to cover the fresh bite mark. After the bite healed, he never shaved it off.

Before he became a cop in 1986, Angel worked at the Empire State Building. This was before terrorist threats, before Homeland Security, and before any of the drum-tight security measures had been implemented at the landmark skyscraper. On the upper floors, the wind sounded like an insistent ghost; closing a door might make another door slam eerily, four or five stories above.

The building also attracted its share of the living who wanted to be specters themselves. "Back in those days, we got one or two jumpers a month," Angel recalls. The real expert suicides, the ones who had done their research, made a beeline for the one spot on the building's Thirty-fourth Street side that ensured their skydive would culminate on the blacktop; any other jumping point would arc the jumper back toward the building, to land on some window ledge. "We could always tell who was going to jump just by the way they looked waiting in line," Angel says. "Their eyes were beady, and they looked like they just weren't there." If security suspected a jumper, they usually hung around in the vicinity, in hopes that the unwelcome company would be a dissuasion.

That ability to read people served Angel well when he joined the New York Police Department in 1986 at the height of the crack epidemic. He was assigned to Manhattan North, and the first time he entered the Thirtieth Precinct, he made the sign of the cross in the hope he'd survive.

"At that time, I had to use my street wise instead of my cop wise, because I wanted to go home alive," says Angel, who grew up on West 125th Street in Harlem, a Puerto Rican kid in the overwhelmingly black projects.

Knowing who is bluffing him is second nature to Angel, and he knew that Maria was lying. Her sister was still inside the house, babysitting Maria's daughter. Over the next few minutes, while the guys were still in front of the house, Angel saw someone pull aside the curtains and peer out the window.

He knew that it wouldn't take much to smoke out the truth, so he had the Rescue Ink guys fan out to ring doorbells and interview neighbors to see if anyone had seen a chocolate poodle being walked around the block.

The story of the poodle that Angel suspected was living behind Maria's door was full of zigs and zags. A woman from New Jersey had e-mailed Rescue Ink about a friend of hers named Liz who had basically given up hope of ever seeing her dog again. A year and a half ago, Liz and her miniature poodle had been visiting a friend in Brooklyn. When someone accidentally left the door open, Chocolate darted out.

Liz spent a few days looking for the dog, but because she was in the military, she had to report for duty in Virginia. While she was out of state, Liz got a call from a Brooklyn bus driver who had found Chocolate and gotten Liz's cell phone number from the dog's ID tags. Liz explained to her that she couldn't come to retrieve her dog, and didn't have any family or friends in the area who could take Chocolate.

Then the bus driver had an idea: She knew a woman in the neighborhood whose daughter had been begging for a dog, but the mother couldn't afford to buy her one. They would be a perfect temporary home for Chocolate until Liz could come and fetch him.

A few weeks later, Angel said, Liz called the woman, who was less than friendly. "I ain't giving you no dog," Maria reportedly told Liz when she called, asking for her dog back. "My daughter is in love with him now, and we won't give him up."

And that's where things had been left—until Rescue Ink came on the scene.

Maria's sister must have called her about the commotion

Rescue Ink was making on the block, because about an hour later Maria came zooming back in her car, supposed party forgotten.

Realizing full well that Angel wasn't buying her story, Maria gave up the pretense and admitted that the poodle was inside.

"'How did you know?'" Angel remembered her asking. "She thought she fooled me."

Maria asked if she could wait until the next day to give up the dog, but Angel knew better; tomorrow she might change her mind. She needed to do the right thing today before she had a change of heart. "Okay. One second—I have to talk to my daughter." Maria sighed. And she asked Angel to come in to help explain things to her nine-year-old daughter.

Angel and Big Ant went inside and talked to the tearful little girl. "Let's do the right thing. No matter how much you love that dog, he isn't yours," Angel said. "You need to do the right thing and give Chocolate back."

"The dog's mommy is outside," Big Ant added. Liz had been waiting in a nearby car. "Come outside and see how much Liz misses him. And if you give him back, we'll bring you a new dog by tomorrow morning."

"Don't make promises you can't keep. She's upset enough already," Maria admonished.

"We'll see you in the morning," Big Ant assured her.

When Chocolate saw Liz, he wriggled in excitement and rushed over to her. Even the child could see it was the right thing to do. Sniffling, the little girl kissed her curly little mocha-colored poodle good-bye.

Every cop has a partner. And Angel Nieves has Cris.

Whenever Angel is at the computer, Cris, his seven-year-old bichon frise, is at his post on the pillow next to the desk. Twice a day like clockwork, the diminutive powder puff bursts into a frenzy of barking and growling as the block's black Labradoodle walks beneath his window. "Don't try it," Angel will warn Cris, who puffs himself up to growl at the black dog's return trip up the block. Then Cris will look at him with big brown eyes and sigh. Like most people, he'd rather not argue with Angel.

Angel gets the Rescue Ink cases that need extra behind-the-scenes legwork, including missing, lost, and stolen animals. Coincidentally, some of his most successful cases have involved little white dogs, just like the one who shares his home and desktop.

Take the case of the missing Malteses. Donna O'Brien was having problems with her water and electricity at her rented home in East Northport, so she checked into a hotel temporarily while her landlord fixed the problems. She had no choice but to leave her six dogs there—two adult Malteses and their four newly weaned puppies—and travel back and forth to care for them. Then, one day, she opened the door and heard . . . nothing. The dogs were gone.

Donna met Rescue Ink at a local diner. "I don't have children," she explained, sobbing from her seat in one of the booths. "I don't sleep at night, I don't know where they are."

Almost everyone had turned out for this case—G, Des, Big Ant, Johnny O, Batso, and, of course, Angel. Moved by her tears, "we told her something you should never say," says

Angel, who hates promising anything he can't deliver. "'Don't worry—we're going to get them back.'"

Donna led them to the landlord's home in the pouring rain. The guys charmed their way past the guard of the gated community, only to find that the landlord wasn't home. His college-age son and daughter were, though. First the daughter came out and asked what they were doing there.

"We ain't going anywhere until we get the dogs," Angel said.

Then the son appeared. "We have no dogs here, so I don't know what you're talking about," he said.

From the interior of the house came some thunderous barking. "That's weird, I hear barking," Angel said.

Sheepishly, the son showed him a huge German shepherd.

"I hear some more dogs down here," shouted G from the driveway of the split-level.

"Unless that shepherd's a ventriloquist, you've got some more dogs," Angel said to the guy.

"I don't know what you're talking about," the son insisted.

"If you're going to lie to me, can you at least brush the white hairs from your shirt?" Angel replied.

Defeated and caught, the son went into the house, returned with one of the adult Malteses, and thrust it into Angel's arms. Then he did the same with the other missing adult dog.

"Where are the puppies?" Angel asked.

"This is all I got," the son replied in exasperation.

Angel was enjoying himself now. "These two dogs are proof that you were in possession of stolen dogs from this rental property of your father's," he said. "I've got evidence now."

"But we did nothing wrong."

"Tell that to the judge."

The son's cell phone rang, and he answered; before the son even spoke, Angel knew it was the father, who the young man must have called when he went into the house the last time. "Daddy, hold on," he said, retreating into the house to finish the conversation.

He came back looking uncomfortable. "The four puppies are back in the rental house—now leave us alone," said the son, slamming the door in the guys' faces.

Sure enough, Rescue Ink found the puppies back at Donna's. No one ever established that the landlord or his family intended to keep the dogs permanently, or determined why they were in their possession in the first place, but it didn't matter. All that did matter was that they were back where they belonged—with their rightful owner.

Rescue Ink has made something of a cottage industry of finding stolen dogs. Some cases are easy, like the two corgis named Daddy Warbucks and Sammy who had been stolen after competing in a New Jersey dog show in March 2008. Hearing the case's details over the phone, Angel deduced that the thieves had really been after the car's GPS system, but when there were no electronics to be found, they nabbed the dwarf-legged herding dogs without calculating just how underappreciated corgis are in terms of supply and demand. A few well-placed inquiries with the shadowy types who know more than the average joe about fencing electronic goods in the Edison, New Jersey, area got the point across: Rescue Ink would be making a lot of noise and some attention-getting inquiries until these dogs resurfaced. Within a day, the two corgis were dropped off at a nearby shelter and reunited with their distraught owner.

Most cases, though, like Clara, the bulldog who started it all, and Mao, a toothless ten-year-old Maltese, require a little more legwork before the dog is recovered.

Mao's owner had left him in her parked Mercedes on Columbus Avenue on Manhattan's Upper West Side while she grabbed a bite to eat. When she returned, she found the window smashed and no sign of Mao. The very legitimate question of why someone would steal an old, wobbly lapdog and leave other things of value in the car—like the coins in the ashtray—isn't something Angel bothers to contemplate, because street logic rarely dovetails with common sense. Mao was likely stolen, Angel shrugs, "because he was there."

Rescue Ink posted flyers offering a $3,000 reward for his return. The word STOLEN was prominent. Soon, a call came in. "A woman called and said she had bought the dog from a crackhead on 129th Street for a few hundred dollars," Angel remembers. A series of subsequent phone exchanges ensued while Angel negotiated a drop-off of the dog.

The location was going to be near the projects on the West Side, and so the guys—Angel, G, Batso, Des, Big Ant, and Johnny O—headed to Amsterdam Avenue, taking up surveillance posts around the block where Angel assigned them. Des, who when he removes his skull rings can look quite unassuming, would go get the dog.

Then Angel's cell phone rang again. The person who had the dog called for a change of plans. The dog would be across town, at 119th Street and First Avenue, near a schoolyard. The guys piled into their rented white van and drove to the East Side. As they did on the other side of town, they took up their places on the street so they could assist Des in case things went awry.

Their presence was soon noted on the block. The drug dealers just assumed the local precinct was working an undercover sting, and they rolled up their sidewalk shops and watched. "Five-O!" they shouted at the Rescue Ink guys, a reference to the "Book 'em, Danno" cops on that vintage crime show.

A woman in her forties got out of a car, clutching a small white bundle. Des approached her and took the dog from her hands. The Rescue Ink guys who had been shadowing Des moved in, and got a jumble of conflicting stories from the woman, who ultimately just left without any reward. "I'm not there to believe," Angel says of all the explanations. "I'm there to get the dog back."

As for Mao, he survived the incident unscathed, with only the loss of the little hoodie jacket he had been wearing.

Growing up, Angel knew he couldn't have any pets. Animals were not allowed in the projects. But there was always room at his *abuela*'s house on 129th Street.

"Every animal we found, we brought there," he says of his grandmother's house. "We even went to the slaughterhouse and stole chickens before they were slaughtered." Angel's grandmother had chickens, roosters, rabbits, dogs, and cats. Whenever he brought a new one, she feigned annoyance, then promptly gave it a bath and added it to the menagerie.

Angel and his friends kept pigeons in a coop atop an abandoned building. Whenever he saw a homing pigeon overhead, he would send up ten or twenty birds from his flock, and the confused bird would descend with them, adding one more to their aviary.

His love for animals has roots in his family tree. Angel's

father grew up on a farm near the coastal city of Rincón in Puerto Rico. In the summer when the family vacationed there, Angel tossed off his shoes, exploring the wide-open spaces, climbing trees to take down fresh mangos and coconuts, and drinking homemade sugarcane beverages. And every summer, Angel would look forward to seeing his *chicherichi*—a handsome rooster that he had first held as a chick in the palms of his hands. But babies have a way of growing up, and Angel's *chicherichi* grew up to be a very famous rooster, a champion in cock-fighting circles. Angel doesn't recall seeing the deadly fights between the enraged roosters, probably because he doesn't want to. His only memory of the pastime is of the island's old-timers, like his grandfather, dressed all in white, going off to see the bloody contests.

He returned to Puerto Rico one summer when he was fifteen, to be told that his beloved rooster was gone. "When they told me, it took four guys to calm me down. My *chicherichi* was dead," he says. "His beak broke"—presumably in a fight, though no one was giving any concrete details—"and he couldn't fight no more." The retired rooster might have lived beyond his glory years. But then, unable to back down from any confrontation, he attacked someone who was sweeping the barn where he lived, and the man defended himself vigorously—so much so that Angel's *chicherichi* wound up in that evening's soup.

"If a person fights, that's their own choice," Angel says. "But getting two roosters to fight or two dogs like pit bulls to fight, the animals don't have a choice there. They can't decide not to fight. This rooster, the one I had, he was my pet. And I never thought he'd end up like that," though to this day he doesn't know exactly who it was that fought him.

As with his *chicherichi*, Angel has no control over the outcome of some of the cases he investigates, which is perhaps the most frustrating part of his job. Some of the cases go beyond the purview of Rescue Ink, and need to be turned over to law enforcement to handle. So Angel does his investigations, fills in as many of the cases' blanks as he can, with names and contact information for complainants, hands them over to police, and then waits while, often, nothing happens.

Angel can tick off the cases he's investigated and documented that he has passed on to law enforcement because they exceed what Rescue Ink can do on its own, only to have them mired in bureaucratic red tape: The guy in Manhattan who advertised that he would find homes for unwanted dogs but instead stole and resold them, likely to research labs. Or the guy in a rural part of eastern Long Island who liked to kill cats by putting them in the dryer, then brag to his girlfriends about it.

Admittedly, a rescue group whose self-described approach to problems is "bing, bang, boom" is also going to have its fair share of near misses. Sometimes they're avoidable, sometimes they're not. Dead ends and unresolved cases come with the territory. But sometimes, cases crescendo beautifully, culminating in endings that Angel couldn't have scripted any better.

The day after they found Chocolate the poodle and returned him to his rightful owner, the Rescue Ink guys pulled up to Maria's house again. Riding with them was a little white poodle. Sugar, who had been saved by a Long Island rescue group, was newly bathed and groomed, with two pink ribbons atop her head.

"When the little girl saw the white poodle, she forgot about the chocolate one," Angel remembers. "Now here she had a dog that she didn't have to hide." And he was pleased that both mother and daughter had learned a valuable lesson: Doing the right thing works out in the end.

Sugar walked into her new home, took a look around, and immediately peed on the rug.

Everyone clapped: To new beginnings.

13

G

Who's the Boss?

G heard the car pull up in front of his house, crunching on the icy January snow. In the back was a crate holding Spike, newly sprung from Eric Bellows's training facility in upstate New York.

It seemed impossible to G that Spike—the dog they had nicknamed "the alligator"—could have made a complete turnaround in such a short period of time. But the assessment Eric had given Joe over the phone when he called sounded good: Eric had pushed all of Spike's buttons, trying to see if he had any hidden triggers. Over and over, Spike proved himself to be totally human-friendly. Eric had even been able to give him a much-needed bath. Spike had no food or toy aggression, and he was so submissive that even a raised voice would flatten him to the ground.

There were just two problems. Because he had lived in his own filth for so long, Spike was having difficulty grasping the concept of housebreaking. And because he was still learning about the world and figuring out where he fit in it, he was showing signs of aggression to the other members of Eric's pack. Whenever Spike got nervous or excited for any reason, he would revert to the behavior he had practiced for so long: running in a short, straight line for several paces, then jumping back in space and doing it again, and again, and again.

What Spike needed was time, and exposure to the world. What he didn't need was placement in a shelter, where the stress of other animals and a small cage would make him return to his previous reactive state of mind.

"The most important thing to keep in mind is to stay calm in all circumstances," Eric had said when Big Ant, Joe, and Junior picked Spike up earlier that day. "For his meals have him sit and wait, so he can focus on being calm before getting what he wants. The more we have him out of that anxious state, the easier it is for him to be the best dog that we know he can be."

Spike was still a work in progress; the challenge now was to build upon the work Eric had begun and add new skills and experience. And he could not be allowed to revert to his old habits and behaviors. That meant he had to go to an experienced foster home, where continued structure would encourage the confidence-building that Eric had begun. Talking it over, the guys soon decided that that home was G's. He had the room, the time, and the calm, confident demeanor to handle a dog like Spike.

G opened his front door and came over to the car, which was spattered with snow and salt from the long drive from the north. The men stood behind the truck as Joe opened the door. Spike looked out expectantly from inside the wire crate.

G had bought a new choke collar for Spike, and as he opened the door to the crate, he slipped it on the dog's neck. Then he let Spike jump out of the crate. Spike dropped his head to the ground to sniff, then looked up to them and wagged his tail hesitantly.

When it comes to making decisions about how to handle and treat dogs, G is an important person to listen to. That's sometimes difficult at the Rescue Ink gatherings, where the loudest voices are usually Ant's and Joe's. G is quiet, but he sees everything. And he has the one quality that is important in dealing with canines of all sizes and breeds: dog sense. Being around dogs your whole life is one thing; paying attention is another. Because he is well attuned to dogs, G can often foresee a problem before it happens, anticipate what a dog is likely to do before he does it. In this way, he's proactive, not reactive.

Until the age of ten, G, who is forty, grew up in the projects in Connecticut. But later, he lived in a more rural part of the state, on a sort of mini-farm with pigs and chickens. "That's where I got my first stitches," he remembers. "I was riding an old boar, and he rode me across a nail sticking out of a post in the barn." G's family had always owned dogs—Doberman pinschers, mostly. His father got their first Doberman as a guard dog for a pool hall he owned. When the billiards business closed, the dog came to live with them, and the breed's sleek, striking presence made an impact on G.

When he moved out on his own, he worked at an aerospace company for two years, then got a job as an industrial firefighter at a chemical plant. Trained to respond to chemical spills, fires, medical calls, and other high-pressure situations, G has a calm, methodical approach that dogs just sense and react to. And G has no problem standing apart from the crowd and doing his own thing: After all, in this crowd of Harley lovers, he rides a Suzuki Hayabusa (for which he takes heaps of good-natured abuse). And he is happy to point out that his "Japanese bike" can hit two hundred miles per hour, leaving the American bikes in the dust.

Like Eric, G is a Rottweiler aficionado. He first encountered the breed in his late teens, when he came across a stray male Rottie while driving down the road. "His head was huge, like a damn lion," G remembers admiringly. He let the dog clamber into his car, then took him to his mother's house. She took one look at the hulking dog and resolved he had to go. Back in the car the dog went. G drove him around the block, and soon came upon a guy who had been out looking for his runaway dog. So G handed the Rottie back to his owner, but he was hooked. The dog had made such a deep impression on him that he knew he would soon have one of his own.

When G was twenty-four, he felt was ready for his first Rottie. But before he even considered looking for one, he decided to educate himself. He wanted this dog to be well trained and under his control at all times, "and if you don't know something, the best way to find out is to read up on it." So G went to the bookstore and bought a book that even today is his bible of dog training: *Good Owners, Great Dogs* by Brian Kilcommons. Today he's on his ninth copy; each time a friend gets a new dog, he lends it out, knowing he'll probably never see it return.

From that book, G learned the training tips that he used on his first Rottweiler, Shabba, and that he still uses today. "I had him well trained," G remembers. To teach him not to stray far from his side, G waited until six-month-old Shabba wandered off in a field, then hid his considerable bulk behind a tree. "That was it," he says; Shabba never again let G out of his sight. "You have to teach a dog to be sociable with people," G says, especially a large and imposing breed like the Rottweiler. "That book helped a lot—it taught me what I needed to do even before I bought the puppy, like how to pick a dog out of the litter," explains G, who has a little trick for marking his pick in the whelping box: He paints the puppy's toenail with a dab of nail polish, so he can find it on his next visit.

As an added precaution, G doesn't allow his dogs to jump up, or even teach them to give their paw. "If your dog tries to shake paw with a little kid, and then knocks him down, you've got a problem."

Brian Kilcommons, who wrote that book almost two decades ago, says it still sells briskly today. While the current trend in dog training is toward "purely positive" training with food rewards, many of the Rescue Ink guys, G included, will use corrections, provided they are fair and appropriate. "The feeling among some trainers is that any type of correction is abuse, and it just isn't true," says Brian. "The key is using approaches that work, never correcting when you are trying to teach something, and not trying to turn into something you're not."

No matter what your training philosophy, G understands that getting a dog is a serious commitment that will last a lifetime: He had Shabba for nine years until he died.

Now G has Boss, his two-year-old Olde English bulldogge, also called a Leavitt bulldog, a breed that was developed in the 1970s. The Olde English is a longer-legged iteration of the classic English bulldog, which has been crossed with bullmastiff and pit bull.

G knew from his research that the smart way to buy a dog of any breed is the time-consuming, old-fashioned way: Take your time, do your research, visit the breeder, and be sure to meet the mother, as well as the sire if possible.

But G's deliberate method is a far cry from the way many people choose a dog. Quite often the decision is made spur-of-the-moment in a pet store: See the cute furry face in the window, fall in love, plunk down your American Express card, and head home with your new responsibility.

Like all the Rescue Ink guys, and more and more people thanks to the group's education efforts, G knows that the vast majority of pet-store puppies come from large-scale breeding establishments informally called "puppy mills." In the mills, females are bred at every heat, as often as every six or eight months. As a rule, because the breeders don't particularly care, the bitches are not screened for health or temperament problems, and they are confined in cages, often under conditions as cramped and filthy as the one Spike was rescued from. Many mill dogs live in wire-bottomed cages, which splay and deform their feet but allow the urine and feces to fall through, sometimes onto the dogs below them.

Rescue Ink has participated in several events to raise the public consciousness about the real story behind that doggie in the pet-store window. The most high-profile of the events they've attended was the fifth annual Puppy Mill Awareness Day march on September 20, 2008, held in the seemingly bucolic countryside of Lancaster, Pennsylvania. The day's events were organized by Hollywood actor Chris DeRose, who has appeared on *General Hospital* and *Baretta*. An ardent animal activist, DeRose has gone undercover to document the misery of puppy mills and has been arrested and jailed for protesting animal cruelty, including in a daytime break-in at UCLA's Brain Research Institute to film its animal-research laboratories. The day centered on a march through Intercourse, Pennsylvania, the center of Amish tourism and a puppy-mill hotbed.

While the nation's largest concentration of mills is in Missouri, Pennsylvania does a brisk business in rearing puppies for sale. According to Puppy Mill Awareness Day organizers, in 2007 Pennsylvania mills sold 124,296 dogs and puppies, with 156,534 remaining at the kennels for breeding. In the Lancaster area, the Amish community, with its deep roots in agriculture and livestock, has traditionally been associated with commercial puppy breeding operations. According to the Lancaster County Humane League, between two and three hundred licensed breeders operate in the county, as well as an unknown number of unlicensed breeders. Commercial pet breeders are licensed by the U.S. Department of Agriculture, the same agency responsible for grading your ground beef.

Almost eight hundred people showed up at 10:00 A.M. at the field where the march started, about double the turnout of previous years' marches. Some people walked dogs—basset hounds, collies, wheaten terriers, pits—whose tongues lolled as the day grew warmer. Other marchers carried banners that said "Puppy Mill Dogs Never Get Out of Jail." Some marchers arrived from miles away in buses chartered by rescue groups specifically for the occasion. Jana Kohl, whose family founded the department-store chain of the same name, adopted a three-legged puppy-mill poodle named Baby whose vocal cords had been cut to stifle her constant cries. That summer, Kohl traveled around the country in a bus to promote her new book, *A Rare Breed of Love*, and to help raise awareness about puppy mills. "Baby on Board," read a yellow sign on the rear of the bus. Then, below it: "We brake for tummy rubs."

"No more puppy mills!" chanted the marchers as they filed along Route 340, the main route through Intercourse. Scenic farms with beautifully manicured fields surrounded them. Occasionally, Amish farmers passed them in their horse-drawn buggies. "They came pretty close to us, but they didn't run us off the road," G says. And besides the near misses by the plain people, "last year, the marchers said they got a lot of abuse from the people driving their cars by."

Not this year. With Rescue Ink as sort of unofficial escorts, the marchers proceeded unimpeded, chanting "No more puppy mills!" and stopping in front of farms known to sell puppies commercially. Many drivers honked their support. Others gave icy stares.

"The most amazing moment for me was at the flea market," G remembers, referring to Kitchen Kettle, an outdoor market that the marchers snaked through, past stands selling home-made jam and elaborately pieced quilts. It was a high-profile place to make the point that puppy milling exists here, despite Lancaster's meticulously marketed image of gentle farmers and well-managed fields. As the marchers at the front of the line exited the market, they passed the end of the line, still going into it. "We just about shut the place down," says G. So the marchers went through a second time, just for good measure.

At the end of that two-hour march, hundreds of people had heard the message about the misery that puppy mills breed. And later, the guys learned that one dog had been delivered from it: Responding to an offer to turn in an old or incapacitated mill dog, no questions asked, one miller handed over a nervous-looking chocolate Lab. Not knowing her name—or if she even had one—the marchers named her Chanel.

G got his last Rottweiler about a year before he got Boss, choosing him from a litter just as he had Shabba. Again, he reread his favorite dog book, and trained the newly named Cain with consistency and follow-through from the minute he arrived home as an eight-week-old puppy.

But no matter how much research and careful planning G did, some things were just out of his control. When Cain was two years old, he looked to be dropping a little weight, and his appetite waned. G took him to the vet expecting a benign diagnosis, like worms, or at worst maybe Lyme disease, a tick-borne infection that is common in Connecticut.

The vet took some X-rays of Cain, and returned with a devastating verdict: Cain had cancer. The vet put the X-ray on the light box on the wall. He showed G the growths that had almost entirely engulfed his Rottweiler's stomach. It was too far gone; there was nothing that could be done.

"Cain, you got cancer," G remembers telling his handsome dog, who looked up at him knowingly, as if he understood. "The vet told me, 'Listen, give him whatever he wants. Make him comfortable,'" G continues. "So I went home, took some steaks out of the freezer, and cooked them for him." Cain had to be hand-fed, but he relished every morsel.

The weeks passed, and Cain withered away from a stout 110 pounds to a sickly 72. G knew the day was coming when he would have to say good-bye. Eventually, about a month after he first heard the word "cancer," he did, laying Cain's thin frame on a soft blanket on the floor of the examining room at the vet's office. Before the vet inserted the needle, Cain laid his head on G's leg, and G rubbed his fur and told him what a good boy he was.

Cain's doghouse had stood eerily quiet since Cain was put down in January 2009. He had had an ample run, fifteen by thirty feet, and a heated doghouse that kept him warm even on the chilliest New England nights. And now Spike was going to take up residence there, temporarily, until G finished his training, and another foster home, or better yet an adoptive one, could be found.

Followed by Ant and Joe, G opened the gate to Cain's old run and took Spike inside. Spike walked around the generously sized chain-link enclosure, exploring. At the farthest end of the run, he stopped, sniffed around, and then pooped. It was progress—he hadn't soiled the crate during the car ride, and had waited to go outdoors.

Next, G showed Spike the doghouse, parting the heavy plastic flaps over the opening to reveal the interior. It was full of fresh, clean hay, and the heat lamp inside made it appealingly toasty. Spike hopped inside, burrowed into the hay. And, then . . . blissful nothing. He wasn't coming out.

"The day we went over to rescue Spike, I was concerned about even approaching this dog. But there's a hundred percent change," G reflected.

His game plan going forward was simple: He'd work with Spike three times a day for short fifteen-minute sessions focusing on basic training such as sit, stay, and heel. He'd also recruit his nine-year-old son to help him feed, train, and walk the dog.

"The kid that we got him from is probably just a little bit taller than my son, so that's probably why he started smelling my son" when he first arrived, G said. "He was probably thinking that it was his owner." And having Quentin work with Spike would reinforce to the dog that kids are to be loved and respected, just like G and the other caring adults he had come to be with since he was rescued from that pen, which seemed like a lifetime ago.

There was a commotion outside the run, and the three men turned to see Boss, G's exuberant bulldog, coming toward Spike's enclosed run. Boss and Cain had been fast friends, playing with each other at every turn, and Boss was clearly eager to kindle a similar friendship with Spike.

But the feeling wasn't mutual. Spike emerged from his house and appraised the snorting, silly bulldog on the other side of the chain link. Then Spike flung himself at the fence in a fury of snarls.

Boss, however, was undaunted. Showing the ultimate sign of canine submission, he rolled on his back, kicking his legs out joyously. Spike again charged the fence, teeth flashing, but Boss just ignored him, rolling himself against the fence.

"Boss, give us a chance to work with Spike," said G in exasperation. Somehow Boss had managed to get a glob of bulldog goober on Spike's head.

"This is the third home for Spike," G said as he let himself and the guys out of the run and closed the latch behind him. "I want his fourth to be his last."

Just a few weeks after Puppy Mill Awareness Day, Rescue Ink got a call from a Long Island high school student. She was in a vet-tech program at her school, and as an assignment, her teacher had asked the class to look at Rescue Ink's Web site.

The teenage student did more than that: She called Rescue Ink's hotline to report her next-door neighbor, a schoolteacher who was rarely home, sometimes away for days at a time. But there was a dog inside. The girl knew it not just because of the periodic barking coming from the house, but also because of the terrible smell that emanated from it.

Johnny O, Batso, G, Joe, Big Ant, and Bruce arrived at the clapboard house to find no one home. At the back of the house, they discovered a bathroom window that was open a crack. They couldn't hear a dog, but they smelled an odor so foul it could have been a decomposing body.

Concerned that there might be a dead something inside, the guys called the local Society for the Prevention of Cruelty to Animals, which persuaded the landlord to come by with a set of spare keys.

The SPCA officers entered the house, and inside the bathroom was a five-year-old French bulldog. She was covered in urine scald because she was forced to stay in the tiny room lying in her own excrement.

At the Pennsylvania puppy-mill rally, Rescue Ink made a contact, one of many, with the French Bulldog Rescue Network. The national group helps get those adorably bowling-ball-shaped dogs out of harm's way. The network had a foster home available on Long Island, but first the frightened little dog had to go to the local shelter, where she was held for twenty-one days in case her owner came to claim her. He never did, and on the twenty-second day she was bailed out of the shelter by the rescue network, which renamed her Freesia, after the sweet-smelling flower. And a day after that, newly bathed and babied, Freesia attended a fancy fund-raiser benefit for Rescue Ink, wearing a baby diaper because she was hopelessly unhouse-trained.

⤳⤳

Being one of a trendy breed that's hard to find and expensive to purchase, Freesia the French bulldog soon found a home. But Spike wouldn't be so easy to place. Part Rottweiler, part pit, with a huge head and a voluminous brindled coat that stood out from his body, he looked something like a hyena, G thought. Unlike Freesia, whose cuteness made up for her shortcomings, if Spike were to find a new home, he would have to be well trained, perfectly socialized, and housebroken.

The day after Spike arrived, G started working with him. Short, frequent sessions were the key, G knew, so he took out a fifty-foot lead and attached it to Spike's collar. The dog walked out of the open run door and ran a few feet to explore G's snow-covered backyard. But he didn't want to stray far—only five or six feet away from G.

G walked Spike to the front of the house and positioned him on the concrete landing in front of the steps to the front door. Then he ran the long lead through the wrought-iron railing, so that he could hold it taut against one of the rails and correct Spike if he moved. Then he moved back to where Spike was standing.

"Sit," said G, and the dog complied.

"Good boy," said G, reaching into his pocket to give Spike a piece of string cheese, Spike's favorite reward, according to Eric.

"Stay," said G, moving a few steps away from Spike. He held the leash against the railing, ready to pull it in case Spike moved.

Seeing G's backward motion, and wanting to follow him, Spike stood up eagerly.

"No," G said evenly, giving the leash a little tug. "Sit."

Spike leaned back on his haunches and sat.

"Stay," G repeated, stepping back again.

This time, Spike didn't move a muscle. G returned to Spike's side and praised him.

After several repetitions, class was over. Slow and steady wins the race, and the same applies to dog training: It is better to end on success, and before the dog gets bored or tired.

Once Spike had mastered a solid stay, G would add distractions, like another dog or person that might cause Spike to break concentration. And once the basic obedience commands that Eric had taught Spike were ingrained, G wanted to teach him to track, just to give the dog a break from the monotony of basic obedience. Herring is G's preferred bait. He ties or tapes a piece of the dried fish to his shoe, then walks across the yard. Because the odor is so pungent, most dogs follow it readily. Soon, Spike would associate the command "Seek!" with putting his nose to the ground, and he would be able to follow any trail once given an article that contained the scent he was to follow.

But Spike was a long way from that right now. Their formal training over for the moment, G returned with Spike to the backyard. Holding Spike on the long lead, G called his son to let Boss out of the house. G wasn't exactly sure how Spike would react, but he knew his Boss. Supernaturally good-natured, the bulldog would just turn and walk away if Spike tried anything impolite. And because Spike was leashed, G would be able to stop him if he truly tried to do Boss any harm.

Boss came bounding out of the house toward G and Spike. His body language was relaxed—loose muscles, tongue lolling, eyes soft and playful. A born canine diplomat, he made sure his approach to Spike was an oblique one: Coming in to greet another dog at an angle is considered good manners. Advancing straight ahead is interpreted at best as rude and at worst as a threat.

Boss slowed up as he approach Spike, and the stubby knot that is his tail vibrated with friendliness. G could see that Spike was tense. The hair on his back stood up—"piloerection" is the scientific name for the reaction. He was wagging his tail, but it was a slow, stiff, pendulumlike motion. His posture radiated tension, but G stayed relaxed and, most important, remembered to breathe. Nothing triggers a dogfight faster than a worried human who holds his breath.

Spike was ready to strike, and he did. He growled and lunged at Boss, but G calmly corrected him. After one more halfhearted attempt, Spike gave up and decided to give Boss the benefit of the doubt.

A few hours later, Angel's cell phone buzzed in the Bronx. So did Eric's and Johnny's and Ant's and Joe's on Long Island. And Batso's in Connecticut, and Des's wherever he was that day. They flipped open their phones and watched the short video snippet that G had sent.

In it, Spike and Boss were gamboling in the snow-covered backyard, playing and chasing each other like old friends.

14

Rebel

Happy Ending

Ⓣhe Piper aircraft taxied up to the hangar at Republic Airport, a small suburban airport in Farmingdale, New York, on the westernmost edge of Suffolk County. Scheduled to arrive from Murray, Kentucky, at 11:30 P.M. on a windy Sunday in February, the plane had been delayed by ice formation on its wings. After landing in Pennsylvania for an hour-and-a-half detour into a heated hangar to melt the ice, the pilot had finally arrived in New York at 1:00 A.M.

Even before his aircraft rolled to a stop, the pilot was eager to be back in the sky. He was far behind schedule, and his sole goal was to drop off his cargo—two muscle-bound men and one strange-looking dog.

The door of the small propeller-driven plane opened, and G emerged, carrying some duffel bags and two sets of noise-blocking headphones. He looked relieved to be on solid ground again, and exhausted after some twenty hours of round-trip flying. It seemed impossible to him that he had left Republic Airport at 7:30 the morning before. It felt like a week had passed.

213

Then Joe ducked out of the impossibly small-looking aircraft. The pilot helped him open a small door on the side of the plane that accessed the cabin. Joe reached in and then leaned in deeper, struggling to remove something from the cabin. Finally, he extracted a medium-size red dog wearing a harness so new it still had its price tag attached. He set the wriggling animal down on the tarmac.

The dog shook himself good-naturedly and wagged his tail. He had very little fur on his face, which was mostly covered with large patches of shiny pink skin. He had no outer ear flaps at all, and his ear canals were so swollen, they bulged out of either side of his head. He looked more like a walrus or a seal than a dog, but that's what he was: Rescue Ink's new clubhouse dog.

On January 31, 2009, an emaciated red-nosed pit bull wandered into a garage in Murray, Kentucky. When the homeowner returned, she found him there, getting along placidly with her own two dogs. He had puncture wounds on his face and neck, and his face was so swollen he looked like a shar-pei. He had once had ears, but they had been cut or torn off, leaving ragged ribbons of cartilage framing his skull. That soon became his temporary nickname: Ribbon.

The homeowner took the dog to the Humane Society of Calloway County, which arranged to have him boarded at a veterinary office, where he was given antibiotics and pain medication. The strips of flesh that were all that remained of his ears were neatly trimmed and sutured. He just needed time—time to gain weight and for the many wounds on his head, neck, and legs to heal.

But Ribbon also needed a home, and that was a far bigger problem. The humane society's executive director, Kathy Hodge, was at a loss over what to do with the obviously abused creature. Her shelter had no expertise in abused pit bulls, and she was reluctant to adopt him out. She also did not want to euthanize him if there was any possibility of getting him the rehabilitation he needed.

Kathy had no idea what Ribbon's story was, and probably never would. She knew that police had busted up a dogfighting ring in a nearby county. Perhaps Ribbon had been turned loose from there. Either way, she had no leads and very few options. So she sent an urgent e-mail out to four reputable pit bull rescue groups that she trusted and respected. One, in Tennessee, forwarded the e-mail to Joe.

"I got the e-mail with the pictures and called Mary," Joe remembers. "I told her to call these people and tell them we would do whatever they needed. Mary said we have no money to give them. I told her I would get it even if I had to steal it. I know what it feels like to be in this dog's situation, left for dead, and not know where to go and who you can turn to. I told her, I want this dog here. I will go pick him up even if I have to drive there by myself."

When the rest of the guys read the e-mail, and saw the pictures of Ribbon, there was an instant connection. He was a survivor, a tough dog who didn't fold. But while he looked more than a little rough on the outside, wore the scars of where he had been and what he had seen, they hadn't changed his basic good nature. He still loved life, and people, and other dogs. He was a walking billboard for both the forgiving, loving nature of pit bulls and the atrocities of the fighting ring.

The challenge was getting him up to New York. A few

weeks before, at a fund-raising rescue benefit in New Jersey, the Rescue Ink guys had met representatives of Animal Rescue Flights, or ARF, a nonprofit group that transports rescued animals, many of them facing death row at kill shelters, to other parts of the country where loving homes await. Ribbon sounded like a perfect candidate, and Mary immediately got on the phone to arrange for his transport to New York.

G and Joe got some sleep after their late-night arrival with Ribbon. Then they headed to the clubhouse, where everyone had assembled to meet the dog they had heard so much about. When the amber-eyed dog walked into the clubhouse, there was an eruption of elation, curiosity, and for some, relief.

"I was afraid I wouldn't be able to look at him," Eric admitted, as Ribbon wagged his tail furiously at him. "He's going to be really good when we go to the schools. I'd like to see these smart-ass kids laugh at him. You can show all the pictures you want, but when you have an actual dog like this to show people what dogfighting is all about, there's no comparison."

The dog's ears looked terrible, with each ear canal so swollen its sides touched. Still, this was a huge improvement over what Ribbon had looked like when he'd been rescued two weeks before. "The ears were so infected," remembers Kathy Hodge, "that when the volunteer drove over to pick him up, he got in the car, shook his head, and pus flew all over her car. She spent the rest of the day cleaning it off."

The closer the guys looked at Ribbon's wounds, the more disturbing his story became: There were thin cuts around his muzzle and legs, suggested that he had had his mouth tied shut and been hogtied.

As Ribbon made his rounds around the room, sniffing curiously and stopping for back scratches and affectionate thumps, G and Joe told the story of their trip: The tight quarters and freezing temperatures in the tiny airplanes. The joyous reception from Ribbon's rescuers when they arrived. The generosity of Ribbon's vet. How Kathy and her humane-society volunteers spent the down time waiting for their delayed plane by rescuing a pig whose ears had been mauled so badly in a probable dog attack that he was Ribbon's oinking alter ego. ("I would've taken the pig back with us," said Joe in all seriousness, "but there wasn't any room on the plane.") How during the flight Ribbon had refused to wear the red coat that Mary had gotten for him, fussing until he eventually wriggled out of it. And how Joe and G had panicked when they tried to rouse the dog and he didn't move. They thought he was sick; he was just in a deep, contented slumber.

At the dark, deserted Kentucky airport the night before, Ribbon was ready to follow G and Joe wherever they led him. "He jumped up on the wing of the airplane like that's what he did," Kathy recalls. "He just looked so comfortable, and he bounced on in there."

During his convalescence at the vet's office, Ribbon became very attached to the vet tech who tended to him every day. He showed absolutely no signs of aggression to humans, and was friendly with dogs, too. "We wondered if there was a situation that could flip that switch and make him angry," Kathy says. But if there was, they never saw any indication that Ribbon was anything less than a sweet, loving dog.

One thing was very clear: Ribbon was extremely food-motivated. His nose was constantly to the ground, looking for morsels. He would sell his soul for a bit of string cheese. This was very good news, as it meant he would be very easy to train.

Then again, Ribbon didn't need much work on his manners. Yes, he pulled on the leash. But he eagerly sat for a treat, and even offered his paw. "This dog was someone's pet before," G said, intently watching Ribbon as he politely took a treat from Johnny O. He was clearly well socialized to people and dogs. He didn't growl or otherwise protest when someone stuck a hand in his food bowl or tried to take away a bone or rawhide. Even sadder than the story of his abuse was the growing possibility that he had once been someone's beloved pet and had been stolen to be used as a bait dog.

Ribbon didn't respond to their calls and whistles, and some of the guys wondered aloud if he was deaf. "When you tell him to sit, he does," said G, rolling his eyes. "How do you figure he can't hear?" The verdict would be in soon enough: Ribbon had an appointment at the vet's office later that afternoon.

Now that Ribbon had met his pack, the next order of business was a new name. While it had served ably as an interim name, Ribbon, everyone agreed, just didn't suit him. As suggestions were tossed out, Junior wrote them on the dry-erase board on the clubhouse wall. "JD," short for Jack Daniel's. "Jim Beam." "Bourbon." Clearly, Ribbon's home state of Kentucky reminded the guys of some powerful hooch. "Cassius" or "Ali," because the famous boxer hailed from that southern state. "Rebel," a classic good-ole-boy name.

The guys put it to a vote, and all except Batso, who abstained, wrote their choice on a piece of paper, crumpled it up, and tossed it in a Styrofoam coffee cup.

Ali had a cluster of votes, then Rebel came on strong. When

all but one of the slips of paper had been read, the two names were neck and neck, at four votes each.

Bruce unfolded the last vote and read it aloud.

Rebel it was, with five votes.

The inspiration was *American Idol.*

On a Sunday afternoon in late February, the Rescue Ink guys—all except G, Batso, and Angel—took their seats behind two adjacent banquet tables in a ballroom at Junior's catering hall, Chateau la Mer. Almost by osmosis, Junior had become the newest Rescue Ink member: Though he didn't have any ink, he had been there for almost all of the rescues in the last two months. Behind the guys, floor-to-ceiling windows over-looked the Great South Bay, where wedding parties often arrived by yacht. Waiting in an adjacent room were about two dozen potential volunteers who had learned about this casting call of sorts from an e-mail and follow-up calls from Mary.

Rescue Ink had always operated with a sort of pack mental-ity, but as its projects grew more ambitious, the need for help at events, at the clubhouse, and behind the scenes in general had become increasingly obvious. The guys had compiled a list of interview questions for the assembled attendees. Some were obvious: What kind of experience do you have with animals? Can you foster an animal? Can you do transport, or work on fund-raising? Some were vaguer: Do you remember the experi-ence that made you love animals so much?

One by one, the prospective volunteers came into the ball-room and handed their applications to Johnny O, who sat at one end of the long table. Some were old hands at rescue.

Others were stay-at-home moms or recent retirees with time on their hands and the yearning to do a good deed. There was Fran, a teacher retired after thirty-three years in the class-room. (When she taught special ed, "I had a lot of guys like you in class," she said matter-of-factly. "I know how to handle you.") There was a twenty-something vet tech who admitted to having been turned down by seventeen vet schools. There was Brian, twenty-three, in an Ed Hardy sweatshirt, who had gotten tattoos of his late dog's actual pawprints. The young-est applicant was ten-year-old Angeline, who stood ramrod straight and answered all the questions with the composure of a Marine. What they all had in common was a genuine love for animals, a desire to help them, and perhaps not a little bit of curiosity about this band of tough guys.

A woman named Lauren had a virtual menagerie in her house: four dogs and four cats, all rescues, and some birds. "I've had pigs, iguanas, lizards, snakes, scorpions," she said, ticking off a veritable phylum. "I lost the scorpion in my room once, and it ended up in the laundry basket." Not surprisingly, Lauren came from a family of animal lovers. "When I was born, my mom had rescued a skunk," she explained. "It used to sleep in the sink."

"Was that an excuse for your mom not to do the dishes?" Ant joked.

When it was his turn, a thirteen-year-old named Dylan talked about the three rescued pit bulls he owned. "There are people who are fighting them that are ruining that breed," he said, running his hand through his crew cut.

"And that's because abusers are . . . ?" said Joe, trailing off expectantly.

"Losers," replied Dylan without missing a beat.

One of the last volunteers was a quiet, petite woman named Donna. She walked up to the edge of the banquet table and handed Johnny O a manila envelope. Inside were pictures of a dog he and the rest of the guys knew well: Freesia the French bulldog, who had been rescued from a filth-covered bathroom. The woman, Donna Guidi of the French Bulldog Rescue Network, had fostered Freesia for the last four months. "Freesia was adopted on Friday," she said, as the guys clapped and cheered. Freesia's new family included two girls, ages seven and ten, "and you guys are their heroes," she said, beaming.

Donna was a dedicated rescuer: She had fostered twenty-six dogs in the last three years, three of them Frenchies, the rest boxers. She had two boxers of her own, one of which was deaf. "He was being bounced around, kept being returned by his new owners," she said. "I needed a reason to get out of bed in the morning. I needed a mission, so to speak, and he really helped me emotionally."

"So he basically rescued you," Junior volunteered.

Donna nodded, smiling. "I was so grateful for what this dog did for me, I wanted to give back." And that is exactly what Rescue Ink is doing, she added. "I'm such a groupie," she said, walking under the sparkling chandeliers and out of the ballroom. "They're the biggest guys, but they have the biggest hearts."

The day after arriving in New York, the newly named Rebel went to see Dr. Dennis Leon, DVM, at Levittown Animal Hospital. Crowding inside the exam room, Joe, G, and Junior got clarity on some things—and a wait-and-see on others.

"I know that he can hear—he definitely responds to sounds,"

Dr. Leon said with finality. He had seen the dog lift his head in curiosity when he heard another dog barking. If he was not responding to the guys when they called, that was likely because he was unfocused, taking in the new sights and smells around him.

Like everyone else who had come into contact with Rebel, Dr. Leon found him almost supernaturally friendly. "If this was your ear that had been cut off and infected, you wouldn't let anyone near it," he said. "He just wants to love, which, unfortunately, is why he was a bait dog."

As for Rebel's swollen ears, only time would tell. "When I looked inside the ear canal, there was a lot of discharge and debris, mudlike stuff," Dr. Leon explained. Also, above Rebel's left ear there was still a lot of scabbing and crusting, and an infection was brewing underneath. Though Rebel had been on a course of antibiotics in Kentucky, Dr. Leon prescribed another round, along with antibiotic eardrops and an ear wash. "Overall, he's really thin," Dr. Leon noted. "You can see his backbone. He weighs fifty-three pounds now, and he's going to need to put on at least another fifteen to get up to a desirable weight."

Because of the extensive scar tissue around his face, much of which had already healed, Rebel's fur might never grow back. "There might not be any hair follicles left," Dr. Leon said, though "the bald spots might get smaller."

Finishing off Rebel's exam, Dr. Leon noted that his teeth were broken and worn, as if he had been chewing on rocks or other hard objects. G mentioned that Rebel had a hoarse bark, and asked if it were possible that he had been debarked—that is, had his vocal cords cut. It was possible, replied Dr. Leon. "He could just have laryngitis from lots of barking, or he could have been kicked in the throat," he explained. If a more normal-sounding bark didn't return, then, yes, he might very well have been debarked.

The guys returned to the clubhouse with Rebel. Bruce had already posted a walking, feeding, and play schedule for Rebel; the guys would take turns working with him, giving him his medicine.

"It's cool to rescue," says Johnny O. "It's not a nerdy thing or inappropriate because a lot of the women do it. If you love animals, you love animals. And it just shows that you don't judge a book by its cover." Just like Rebel. And just like Rescue Ink.

In the days and weeks after his arrival, Rebel continued to impress the guys with his even temperament and general love of life. His biggest vice was his appetite for cats, about which he was clearly unrepentant. He would sit outside the door to the clubhouse's cat room, stonily determined. This wasn't Rebel's fault; it was a hardwired part of being a pit bull, which has a naturally strong prey drive. But try explaining that to the cats.

When Rebel first arrived, dog trainers came out of the woodwork, offering to train him. Most used punishment-based methods, like shock collars or physical corrections. Many of the Rescue Ink guys are old-school when it comes to dog training; they learned how to communicate with their dogs with the "jerk and pop" choke-collar techniques made popular in the 1950s by returning World War II dog trainers. But Rebel had been through so much that they wanted the gentlest training method possible. And Rebel really didn't need that much remedial work, just some brushing up on his basic manners. Most important, for Rebel's progress, the guys needed to come to a consensus on how they would train him.

For their first foray into positive dog training, the guys got in touch with Denise Herman of Empire of the Dog in Brooklyn. Denise had trained at the San Francisco SPCA Academy for Dog Trainers, known as the "Harvard for dog trainers."

Eric, G, Joe, Big Ant, Angel, Johnny O, Mary, and Bruce cleared the main room of the clubhouse, pushing all the chairs against the wall so Denise would have room to work. As she stood in the clubhouse, surrounded by this muscled assemblage, she started off with an appropriate analogy: bodybuilding.

"Say you want to get into shape, so you go to a gym, grab a ten-pound weight, do your reps, and go home. If you come back the next day and I throw you a hundred-pound weight, you're going to fail," she said. "That's not because you're spiteful, or because you didn't want to. It's because you haven't worked up to that level yet." Similarly, with dogs, learning obedience is about repeating training, in increasingly more distracting environments, until the dog has the "mental muscle" to respond the way his handler wants him to.

Rather than correcting Rebel with a pop of his collar when he was doing something wrong, Denise showed the guys how to point out when he was doing something right with a well-timed use of the word "Yes!" After distributing a handful of dog treats to everyone in the room, Denise had the guys take turns calling Rebel's name, then saying "Yes!" just as he turned his head in their direction, followed by a food treat. Rebel soon learned the point of this round-robin game, and as the guys called him from different directions, his responsiveness to his name grew faster and faster.

While Denise used food treats, a reward can be anything a dog wants that a human has control over. After the name game, Rebel was thirsty, but instead of giving him his water bowl right away, Denise used it as leverage to teach Rebel how to stay. Holding the water bowl at waist level, Denise waited for Rebel to sit. Then slowly, she lowered the bowl. As soon as Rebel stood, she raised the bowl. When he sat, she lowered it. Up, down, up, down, in ever smaller increments Denise withdrew the water as Rebel broke his sit, then lowered it when he leaned back on his haunches, until the bowl had reached the ground. Understanding now that his waiting got the water bowl where he wanted it, Rebel sat patiently. Without even a word of instruction, he had mastered the sit-stay. And with an enthusiastic "OK," Denise released him, and he slurped the water contentedly.

Sitting around the circle, the guys were impressed. "You could see the dog *thinking*," said Joe in genuine amazement. "He was trying to figure out how to manipulate her, while she was really manipulating him."

When Eric went home that day, he tried the water bowl technique on his min pins. So did Mary with her little yapping pack. And Joe did the same with Bond. It worked.

You can teach old dogs new tricks. And sometimes you can teach their owners, too.

Rebel was transformed. It was just three weeks after his arrival, but this was a different dog from the one G and Joe had brought back on that cold, bumpy flight from Kentucky.

In defiance of the vet's prognosis, Rebel's hair had grown back, even around his ears. With daily cleaning and medication, his ear canals had shrunk almost back to normal. His ribs and spine no longer poked painfully through his skin, and with his weight gain his chest had filled out. He never did recover his ability to bark.

Rebel experienced snow for the first time soon after he arrived at Rescue Ink. At first he had to be coaxed out of the door. "When he stepped into a world of freshly fallen snow, a world that lacked all the smells he was looking for, he was really disoriented," says Bruce. But, true to form, Rebel eventually waded out into the cold white stuff and decided it wasn't that bad after all.

Rebel's story is still a work in progress. Though he was intended to be a clubhouse dog, his life since his arrival has been a series of sleepovers at different Rescue Ink homes. He spent some nights at Joe's, getting introduced to Bond. And of late Bruce has snuck him into his apartment, despite the no-pet lease and the cranky landlady. "I feel like a teenager sneaking a girl in and out of the house," Bruce admits. Forget clubhouse dog; Rebel deserves a permanent home of his own. And what everyone knows is that eventually, he will go to one of the guys' homes and just never leave.

On a balmy Saturday in early March, the first springlike day of the year, Rebel attended his first Rescue Ink event: an adoptathon for the Center Moriches cats in a firehouse party room in North Bellmore. Half a dozen of the volunteers from the "audition" had turned out in their black Rescue Ink staff T-shirts, helping to set up crates and collate adoption forms.

Everyone who went in to see the row of cages of contented, snoozing clubhouse cats stopped to pet and fawn over Rebel.

"It's amazing that even with all this dog has been through, he's like this with people," said John Warkala of North

Bellmore, who was waiting to adopt a calico cat named Pumpkin. "I know I wouldn't be."

And that is the magnetic attraction of not just Rebel, but Rescue Ink as well. Think what you will of them, these guys are proof that a fresh start is possible for anyone, that redemption is attainable. Even if you have a rap sheet, even if you've got a past that needs a fair share of redacting before it's ready for prime time, you can re-create yourself.

But no one teaches this lesson more eloquently or explicitly than the animals. They live in the now, react to each other and those around them based on who and where they are in the moment. For Spike, or Gracie, or Nike, or any of the animals Rescue Ink has taken from an iffy situation, the past is just that: the past. What matters most is how they have changed, and who they are in the process of becoming.

"Animals don't care what you look like. They don't care what color you are. They don't care how big you are, what you do for a living, how much money you make," Joe says. "It's unconditional love. We try to teach animals, but *we* should take a lesson from the animals and try to live our lives like they do, not to judge anybody. The world would be a better place."

For Rebel, and the dozens upon dozens of other animals that Rescue Ink has saved, it already is.

Resources

You wouldn't be reading this book if you didn't love animals. But when you want to provide a great home for a new animal companion, love isn't enough. You also need the knowledge to ensure that you are doing the right thing for the animal you care about, and the resources to find the best care and help you can. Whether you are thinking about bringing a new animal into your home, looking for ways to help an abused animal in your neighborhood, or trying to find a stolen or lost animal, you need to stop, think, and plan.

Here are some of the questions Rescue Ink gets asked every day. The people who ask them have their hearts in the right place; all they need are the facts to get their heads in alignment as well. Remember: The better prepared and informed you are, the less likely you are to have problems.

How do I report abuse?

It's difficult to stand by while an animal is neglected and suffering. No matter what your concern—a dog with inadequate

229

food or shelter, or a cat that you think is being tormented or tortured by someone in the neighborhood—the first step is understanding what protection your local laws and ordinances provide.

Animal cruelty—which includes "passive" forms of neglect such as not providing adequate water or medical care—is not covered by federal law; each state makes its own laws, and establishes the severity of the punishment. For example, in New York, where Rescue Ink does most of its rescue work, as in most states, animal cruelty is a felony, which carries a far stronger penalty than a misdemeanor. For a state-by-state chart, see www .pet-abuse.com/pages/cruelty_laws.php.

Some municipalities have animal-cruelty officers with the power to investigate or arrest animal-abuse cases. (To check a state's anticruelty investigatory-arrest powers, visit www .aspca.org/fight-animal-cruelty/report-animal-cruelty.html.) If your state statute does not permit "animal cops," you can report complaints to local law enforcement. Police officers have the authority to enforce animal-cruelty laws, though some, sadly, do not enforce them. At that point, it is up to you to be persistent and thorough in your insistence that your complaints be followed up on.

Remember, too, that laws can only outline the minimums required of owners, not the ideal. As hard as it may be to accept, an owner who keeps his dog living outside tethered to a doghouse may be fulfilling the minimum legal requirements set out by state law, provided that the shelter meets certain specifications.

In many cases, a positive approach works best with owners, just as it does with their animals. If someone is leaving a dog out with inadequate shelter, judging the person will likely only cause her to become defensive. Instead, you can offer to help better winterize the doghouse, or find a trainer, if the dog's lack of socialization is what is keeping him outside.

Of course, use common sense: If you have any indication that the encounter will turn unpleasant or hostile, do not engage, and make a report on the suspected abuse to the authorities.

What's the best way to get a new companion animal?

Sometimes new additions fall into our laps. But in other cases, we can't wait for serendipity, and are eager to begin the search for a new household companion. Below, in descending order, are the best avenues for obtaining furry, or not-so-furry, friends.

FIRST CHOICE: RESCUE

As its name says pretty clearly, Rescue Ink is about rescuing animals in need. And before you go out and buy a puppy, kitten, bird, or any other animal, you should seriously think about adopting one from a shelter or rescue group.

Rescued animals aren't "broken" or "inferior." If anything, oftentimes it's their former owners who were. Rescued animals have limitless reservoirs of love and affection to give the person who offers them a forever home. Sure, some might require time and patience to forget the experiences that they have had at the hands of loser abusers. But unlike people, animals don't hold grudges. They don't stand in the way of their own healing. And they don't judge. They live in the moment, in the here and now, not in the past or the future.

Rescue animals also have advantages: While puppies and kittens are certainly available at shelters, many adolescent and adult animals find their way there once their "newness" has worn off. Puppies and kittens are cute, but they are a lot of work. The average puppy, for example, only has one hour of bladder control for every month of age. That means that a two-month-old puppy needs to go out *every two hours*. Do you have that kind of time and patience? And once housebreaking is behind you, there's the gnawed furniture and destuffed pillows of adolescence to deal with. Adult rescue dogs are often obedience trained and housebroken. And you will have the satisfaction of knowing that you have given a home to an animal that was in dire need of one.

If you have your heart set on a purebred dog or cat, that doesn't mean you have to go to a breeder. An estimated 25 percent of shelter dogs are purebreds. Nearly every breed has a national and/or regional rescue group that can help you determine if the breed is right for you, and then help you adopt a new forever friend. Purebred cats also find their way into shelters, and breed-specific rescues exist for them, too.

If you want a more exotic pet, they have their own rescue groups, too. Tortoises, rabbits, ferrets, chinchillas ... the list goes on and on. Google the species of animal and the word "rescue" and you will find lots of possibilities. Don't be constrained by geography, either: Many rescuers have wide-ranging transport networks of people willing to put in the miles if it means an animal will get a forever home.

And while it's cool to want to save an animal, remember that you still need to keep your lifestyle and family needs in mind before adding any new animal to your household. If you are older and perhaps less active, opt for a cat or smaller dog.

If you have children, make sure you select a dog whose breed and individual temperament are well suited to tolerating youngsters. If you are thinking about other species of animals, remember that some, such as hamsters, are nocturnal, and may be just gearing up for fun and frolic when you're ready to turn out the lights.

For potential dog owners, it's a good idea to hire a trainer or dog behaviorist to accompany you to the shelter to help make your choice. These professionals are good judges of canine body language, and they know the exercise and time requirements of various breeds. Their input in making a choice of dog is often well worth the cost of a consultation fee.

If you obtain your animal through a private rescue group, they will likely already have a good sense of how the animal behaves and the ideal home for him. As a bonus, the animal might already be living in a foster home, and you can get a report from the foster family about how well he does in the house, and what his strengths and weaknesses are.

If you work all day and have little spare time to spend training and socializing, get some fish.

NEXT BEST CHOICE: REPUTABLE HOBBY BREEDER

If you have your heart set on a purebred puppy, go to a reputable breeder! Prospective owners hear this mantra all the time, but many are confused at just what makes a breeder "reputable."

Good breeders see themselves as stewards of a breed: It is their goal to leave the breed in better shape than they found it. This means not breeding animals with unstable temperaments. It means doing the appropriate health tests to make sure they are not putting animals into the gene pool that have identifiable health problems. And it means taking responsibility for every dog they bring into the world.

While the term "reputable breeder" is used most often with dogs, it's almost always best to acquire any animal, whether canary or chameleon, from a small, home-based breeder rather than a pet store, which usually buys from large-scale farms. While such "cottage businesses" are not automatically disreputable, it's a safer bet to buy from someone who reared the animal him- or herself than from a teenage sales clerk at a pet store.

Here are the signs of a good breeder (for dogs, anyway):

- **A good breeder wants to meet and interview you.**

Most reputable breeders require that they meet the entire family before they sell a dog. So going the "surprise" route probably isn't a great idea. Also, there is usually a wait for a well-bred dog—it could be as much as six months to a year after you do your initial research and decide on a breeder.

Many breeders will not sell to families with children under age five because puppies and preschoolers can often be an overwhelming combination. And some who breed toys and terriers may require the household's children to be even older, due to the physical fragility or temperament of their dogs.

If a breeder balks at selling you a dog, put your emotions aside and listen: What she is telling you is that your lifestyle or family situation might not be conducive to owning the breed right now. Good breeders *never* push a bad match.

Some prospective owners get a little miffed when rescue groups and reputable breeders insist on "interviewing" them before they commit to placing a puppy with them. The flip side of this, however, is that responsible rescuers and breeders will take back any dog they place—no questions asked—no matter what the age or situation. Pet stores and most backyard breeders, unfortunately, do not provide such a safety net.

- **A good breeder sells pet dogs on mandatory spay-neuter contracts.**

Reputable breeders recognize that not every puppy should contribute to the breed's gene pool. Perhaps the puppy has a correctible problem, such as a retained testicle, or an overbite. The puppy might have a cosmetic fault—such as the wrong color or markings. The breeder might feel the puppy will grow up to be too big or too small, or has some conformational fault, like an improperly carried tail.

These "pet-quality" puppies will grow up to be just as healthy and loving as their show-bound brothers and sisters, but they should not be bred. A good breeder will require you to sign a contract stating that you will have your pet-quality puppy spayed or neutered at the appropriate time, which you should determine in consultation with your vet.

Some breeders go a step further and sell such puppies on a "limited registration." These puppies are AKC registered and can compete in all AKC events, including obedience and tracking, for example, but they cannot be shown. If they are bred—against the breeder's wishes—their offspring cannot be registered with the AKC, even if the other parent has full registration.

- **A good breeder is a safety net for the rest of the dog's life.**

Purebred dog breeders face a knotty ethical dilemma: How can they bring more canine lives into the world when so many others are facing euthanasia at kill shelters? To ensure that they do not add to the population problem, reputable breeders take responsibility for every dog they bring into the world, regardless of the situation of the dog, regardless of its health or age.

For this reason, reputable breeders are very careful whom they sell dogs to. While life is not predictable, and changes do happen, such as an unexpected death or a divorce, they want to maximize the chance that every puppy's home is a "forever" one.

• A good breeder does health testing.
Every breed of dog, no matter how generally healthy, is predisposed to certain health problems. To find out what they are, visit the Web site of the breed's parent club, which you can find by Googling the breed name and the words "parent club."

Once you know what the most common health problems are in the breed, find out what tests are available to identify dogs that may have these issues. And in many cases—hips being a prime example—it is not enough for the breeder to say that his vet has looked at a set of X-rays and pronounced them "just fine." Instead, reputable breeders seek out independent, accredited registries that use impartial specialists to analyze and grade test results. (See box on the following pages.)

• A good breeder is not in it for the money.
Reputable dog breeders do not breed in order to help defray their kids' college tuition or pay for that upcoming kitchen renovation. Instead, they invest a significant amount of time and money—from the cost of health testing to the stud fee (which as a rough rule of thumb is equivalent to the cost of one puppy) and time off from work to tend to newborns for the first week or two, to ensure they are not squashed by their mother.

Here are some health problems commonly found in dogs, and how breeders try to identify and prevent them.

Hip dysplasia. This is a persistent problem affecting Labrador retrievers and many other large breeds. Make sure that the sire and dam of your puppy have had hip X-rays done and submitted to a respected health registry such as the Orthopedic Foundation for Animals, OFA (www.offa.org), or the University of Pennsylvania's PennHIP program (www.pennhip.org).

It is *not* enough for a breeder's vet to simply do radiographs and assess them herself; those X-rays must be submitted to the registry's independent experts, who grade them. The breeder should be able to show you the official certificate from OFA or PennHIP documenting the parents' hip status. Again, saying the dog's hips have been vet-checked is meaningless—you want documentation and certification.

Obviously, a puppy whose parents both have hips graded "excellent" by OFA is a better risk than one with no family screening at all, but also look at the whole family history: A dog with excellent hips whose siblings or aunts and uncles were dysplastic is not as good a risk as a dog with excellent hips whose entire family tree is crowded with goods and excellents.

The OFA also screens for other orthopedic disorders such as **elbow dysplasia** (a crippling problems in breeds like Rottweilers and Bernese mountain dogs) and **luxating patellas** (essentially, "trick knees" that pop out of their sockets, a common occurrence in some terrier and toy breeds).

Heart problems. Unfortunately, some breeds are predisposed to genetic heart anomalies that can curtail their life spans and activity levels. Boxers are prone to a form of cardiomyopathy that shows no symptoms until the dog suddenly collapses. Newfoundlands face the risk of subaortic stenosis, in which the presence of extra tissue below the aortic valve impedes blood flow. And Cavalier King Charles spaniels can develop late-onset mitral valve disease.

All these heart disorders are different, but the way breeders involved with at-risk breeds address them is the same: They screen their dogs' hearts and obtain a cardiac clearance from OFA. As with hips and elbows, OFA will issue a certificate pronouncing the dog free of cardiac disease. While this does not mean that the dog cannot produce the defect if bred, it does reduce the risk appreciatively.

Eye problems. Ophthalmological defects affecting many dogs range from progressive retinal atrophy (night blindness) to juvenile cataracts. Breeders can check that their breeding dogs have healthy eyes by having an ophthalmologic exam done every year by a board-certified specialist. Dogs that pass the exam receive a certificate from the Canine Eye Registration Foundation, or CERF (www.vmdb.org/cerf.html).

Thyroid problems. Hypothyroidism, or underactive thyroid gland, is a common metabolic problem in dogs that, once diagnosed, can be treated by medication. Breeders can identify hypothyroid dogs with a blood test. Because hypothyroidism can manifest at any time in a dog's life, many breeders with at-risk breeds retest annually.

Genetic testing. As geneticists learn more about the dog genome, and the genes that cause particular disorders, certain tests are developed that can identify dogs that are carriers for a particular disease. Unlike the tests listed above, which can determine if a potential breeding dog is affected with the disease, DNA marker tests can look inside the dog's DNA and see if it is a carrier for a given disease; carriers are healthy themselves, but can produce the disease in their offspring.

WORST CHOICE: PET STORES

Never mind that puppy in the window.

No matter how cute or cuddly, pet-store puppies most likely come from puppy mills—commercial establishments where the breeding dogs live in cages and are essentially treated like livestock.

Females are bred on every heat cycle, with no rest between litters. Often dogs live on wire—it is easier for cleanup, though it causes painful splaying and sores on the pads of their feet. Puppies are often shipped out for sale at very young ages, sometimes as young as six weeks, even though experts recommend that they stay with their mothers and littermates until eight weeks, so they can learn about bite inhibition and appropriate social interaction with their own kind. (Reputable breeders of toy dogs often keep them until twelve weeks, because they mature so slowly.)

Pet-store owners frequently tell their customers that their puppies come from "reputable" or "hobby" breeders. But such breeders would never allow one of their puppies to go to a new home without their approval, and they would never sell to a "middleman."

When you buy a pet-store puppy, you know nothing about the health or temperament of the parents. You have no connection to the breeder of the dog, no resource to go to if you have questions or problems a few months or years from now. But perhaps most important, when you buy a pet-store puppy, you contribute to the demand for puppy-mill-bred puppies, and add to the cycle of misery of mill-owned breeding dogs.

And you will pay just as much—if not more—as you would for an exceptionally well-bred dog from a hobby breeder.

Some dogs purchased from pet stores go on to fuel the "backyard breeder" phenomenon. "Backyard bred" puppies are produced by individuals who are just casual breeders. They often advertise through local newspapers, or sometimes online. At least such puppies are usually raised in a home environment, which is much better than the impoverished social start their puppy-mill-bred counterparts receive. But "backyard breeders" are often woefully ignorant about the breed they are raising. Being total novices themselves, backyard breeders do not do health screenings, offer no guarantees, and certainly do not take a dog back if things are not working out.

A new wrinkle on the puppy-mill problem is the burgeoning number of puppies from overseas puppy mills, particularly Eastern European countries such as Hungary. Unscrupulous individuals import these puppies into the States, with little regard for the temperament or health of their parents. Then they sell them through pet stores or, increasingly, online puppy-selling sites or newspaper ads.

If in doubt, see if the breeder or owner fulfills the criteria of a reputable breeder outlined in this chapter.

The biggest lure of pet stores is that you can buy what you want when you want it. But a puppy isn't a pocketbook or a pair of jeans. It's a living, breathing creature that shouldn't be acquired on impulse. Don't fall into the trap of "love at first sight," or wanting to "rescue" a puppy from the loneliness of its pet-store cage. Any money you give to a pet store simply gives puppy millers the financial incentive to keep producing more puppies.

How do I find a lost animal?

It's the worst sensation in the world: That sinking feeling in the pit of your stomach when you realize your companion animal has run off or gotten lost. In all cases, time is of the essence.

FOR CATS, TIGHTEN YOUR SEARCH.

Cats are intensely territorial and rarely stray from their home turf, especially those that have been kept indoors all their lives. They also are far less likely to be picked up by a well-meaning stranger. So in lost-cat cases, be sure to scour your immediate area, including under decks and in dense shrubbery, to make sure your cat isn't hiding right under your nose.

For cats that are particularly timid or may be injured or ill, borrow or rent a humane trap to see if you can capture your runaway by luring her in with the enticing aroma of a favorite food or treat.

FOR DOGS, EXPAND YOUR RANGE.

Unlike cats, dogs have true wanderlust. They can be miles away in mere minutes, and it is not unusual for a lost dog to go fifty miles or more afield. Also, Good Samaritans tend to pick up lost dogs, which means your dog might be an inadvertent hitchhiker and cross state lines within hours.

MAKE FLYERS, FLYERS, AND MORE FLYERS.

Post them in high-traffic places such as supermarkets, dry cleaners, and delis. Slip the flyers into inexpensive plastic sheet protectors so they will not get wet, wrinkled, or otherwise destroyed by the outdoor elements.

Don't just focus on your own neighborhood or town: Post the flyers in neighboring areas. Remember, your dog can easily turn up dozens of miles away.

Be sure to include your phone number and a good-quality photo of your cat or dog. If you don't have a photo, use one that is as similar as possible. If you plan to offer a reward, do not list the amount.

CONTACT YOUR LOCAL SHELTER.

Better yet, drop by with a flyer and make a personal connection with the staffers there. Also visit shelters in neighboring communities in case your dog is turned in there. Even if your animal has identifying information such as a collar or microchip, be proactive: Collars can be removed or fall off, and some shelters may miss a chip when they scan new animals, or forget to look for them at all.

SEEK MEDIA ATTENTION.

Call local newspapers and television and radio stations to try to get them to publicize your lost animal. Be polite but persistent in getting their attention.

CONSIDER A PET DETECTIVE.

Pet-recovery services do exist, though they are relatively expensive, since professional searchers often need to transport themselves or their dogs to your community.

Don't waste your time calling K9 and search-and-rescue

dogs in your area. Such dogs are trained not to "critter," or follow other animal scents, when they are working, lest these distract them from finding the humans who are their primary focus. You need a dog that has been trained specifically to search for other animals.

For a good starting point, visit www.lostapet.org.

CHECK ADOPTION SITES.

There is a possibility that your dog or cat might have been taken in by a rescue group. Check in daily at Petfinder.com, one of the largest and most trafficked sites, to make sure your dog or cat is not listed there.

INVEST IN AN OUNCE OF PREVENTION.

Hopefully, your dog or cat will never be lost. But there are important steps to take to make sure he or she will be found more easily if that ever happens. Make sure to microchip your animal, and take a good-quality photo in case you ever need it for identification purposes.

How can I help animals in need?

You don't have to get a tattoo and devote yourself to animal rescue to make a difference in the lives of animals in need. Every little bit of effort and time helps.

VOLUNTEER AT YOUR LOCAL SHELTER.

Spending even an hour a week walking or training shelter dogs can have a powerful ripple effect. Well-exercised dogs are less

likely to develop neurotic habits such as tail-chasing or spin-
ning, which can happen in dogs that are kenneled for too long.
Also, because calm, obedient dogs are more adoptable, spending time teaching a dog basic manners can literally mean the
difference between a new home or the unthinkable.

DONATE TO YOUR SHELTER.

Money isn't the only thing shelters need. Good-quality food,
toys, beds, treats, towels for bathtime, and warm blankets are
all appreciated by shelter cats and dogs. If your beloved pet has
recently passed away, donating his toys and possessions to a
shelter is a great way of honoring his memory.

MAKE YOUR OWN ANIMAL A MODEL CITIZEN.

Most of our nation's problems with animal overpopulation,
neglect, and abuse stem from a lack of responsibility. The
American Kennel Club offers a Canine Good Citizen (CGC)
certification that demonstrates that a dog has passed a test
of basic manners such as sitting, staying, accepting the touch
of a stranger, and reacting well to crowds. Especially if you
own a large, powerful breed, having a CGC demonstrates that
breed-specific stereotypes are just that—stereotypes that make
blanket assumptions.

TEACH YOUR CHILDREN WELL.

Tolerance and respect for animals are learned in your home. If you
treat your cat or dog as a member of the family, your children will
follow suit. Instilling a love of the world around them—including
animals—is the greatest gift you can give the next generation.